THE GROUND OF INDUCTION

THE
GROUND
of
INDUCTION

DONALD WILLIAMS

NEW YORK
RUSSELL & RUSSELL · INC
1963

PREFACE

This is an essay in philosophy. It explores one of those intimate and immense problems which affect every man's specialty as well as his general vocation as man — in the present case, nothing less than the foundations of empirical knowledge and the ultimate difference between warranted and unwarranted belief. As any philosophical essay should, it borrows from the minor sciences where they are accessible and helpful. It borrows most from statistics, pure and applied, for that is the science which has been most nearly exercised with our problem. Its borrowings, however, are too elementary to cause distress to the person who until now has known nothing of the subject. I naturally do not attempt to contribute anything to statistics except philosophical understanding of its foundations, and the only formulas which I employ, or could employ, are no more than can be readily grasped by a diligent ignoramus. Philosophy itself, of course, has its technicalities and abbreviations without which it would take forever to get to its points. Professional students of philosophy are aware of the technicalities, and know better than most people how to get the juice out of a philosophical orange. The interests and abilities of those students I have borne especially in mind. Nevertheless I hope that the timeliness and urgency of this question will recommend it to persons who are philosophers only as all men who would live the examined life are philosophers. Curious and serious people in every profession, or in none, given only a little innocence and application, will be able to appreciate the problem which is here posed and to mull over the solution which I offer.

For persons without special interest in the detail of debate, the main issues are sufficiently discussed, with a minimum of dispute, in Chapters 1, 2, and 4. Chapter 5 works out the implications of our principal conclusion for the theory of scientific method, and Chapter 6 does the same for various important parts of the rest of philosophy. Chapters 3 and 7 are more contentious, the former treating of objections to the prosaic theory of probability here employed, and the latter of objections to the crucial application of the theory to induction. Chapter 8, finally, summarizes our results in the context of other current opinions about the subject. In the three chapters last named I have been at special pains to anticipate and allay the compunctions which the scrupulous philosopher or logician is most likely to feel with respect to the supposedly cardinal ideas of equiprobability, 'indifference', and randomness.

On the academic side, I confess, there is a certain danger in this sort of account of a border-line topic like the validity of inductive inference, that it will fall between the two stools of purely logical or mathematical interest and the more properly philosophical. The statistical logician may be impatient with its arithmetic as elementary and obvious, while the general reader and the polite philosopher are irked and bewildered by what technical gear it does employ. Just here, I think, however, is the root reason why the justification of induction has remained problematic: while the statisticians have not known what is wanted, the philosophers have not known what is to be had. I aspire, therefore, to introduce just enough of the concepts of statistical arithmetic to interest the statistician in the wider significance of the theorems with which otherwise he is far better acquainted than I, and to convince the philosophical inquirer that the apparatus of the statistician, which he may investigate *ad libitum* in the standard texts, provides principles necessary and sufficient for meeting the most important problem of the theory of knowledge.

I have made here as few innovations in terminology as the cause of clarity permits. With respect to punctuation, in a province where usage is not thoroughly standardized, I have chosen from current practices a combination of conventions in the use of quotation marks which is less familiar than it should be. First, I use ordinary double quotation marks when I strictly intend only to name the word or phrase thus enclosed, and not to mention or assert what it designates. Secondly, I use single marks, not for a quotation within a quotation (a nearly useless provision), but for the frequent sort of semi-quotation in which, while genuinely using the quoted word or phrase to designate an object or to assert something, we use it with a leer, so to speak, calling attention to the expression itself, because it is an odd one, or because the author disclaims responsibility for the attachment of the word to its present sense, or because it is an apt phrase for which the author disclaims credit. All punctuation marks other than quotation marks I place outside the quotation marks, except in those rare instances when the marks are truly a part of the expression which is quoted. These uses do not diverge enough from the ordinary conventions to be stumbling blocks, and they are nearly indispensable to any clear discourse about discourse.

I list no acknowledgments to embarrass the friends whose acute arguments over bags of marbles and the morrow's sunrise have helped to give shape to this discussion. I record my thanks, however, to the patient Guggenheim Foundation, for a grant which contributed in its season to this and to other work still in process.

D. W.

November 1, 1945.

CONTENTS

ix

THE GROUND OF INDUCTION

1

THE PROBLEM OF INDUCTION

Induction is the kind of inference which discovers or proves a general law, like *All crows are black*, from an examination of instances of it, such as a set of black crows. By induction we conclude that the sort of thing which has happened in such and such circumstances up to now will continue to happen in similar circumstances. By induction of an elementary variety we infer that since water has quenched our thirst before, it will do it again, or that since all the stony meteorites which we have examined have contained chondrules, the rest have them. By induction, again, only superficially disguised, we infer that because the Einstein theory, or the theory that the kitten has been in the work basket, is borne out by all the evidence so far available, it will likely continue to be borne out by further evidence, and is indeed probably true. All our knowledge outside the self-evident truths of logic and mathematics, like $5 + 7 = 12$, and the self-evident truths of sense experience, like *This is white*, is confirmed directly or indirectly by the processes of induction, and there are philosophers who dispute even those exceptions.

The humblest animal can in some wise learn from experience, and the rationality supposed to set man above the rest of the animal kingdom consists chiefly of a refinement and elaboration of this power. The intelligent man differs from the dolt, as the scientist in his specialty differs from the intelligent layman, by his facility with the devices of induction. Every schoolboy knows that we know today immensely more than the ancients because we have learned to learn, systematically and self-consciously, from experience. In official metaphysics and morality, and sometimes in politics, we commonly reject the inductive procedure with more or less atrocious results, but our scientists, our inventors, and our industrialists in their mundane fields have won triumphs beyond compare by means of a purified discipline of observation and hypothesis. Less formally than the physicists, but on the same principles, the physician, the lawyer, the detective, construct their diagnoses and confirm them by the data of sensation and experiment, while the man of affairs, the housewife, the farmer, and everybody else, survive or perish, prosper or fail, so far as they have the same knack. The Brahman, on the other hand, who believes that an enemy who learns his real name will have magical power over him, or the citizen of a feudal state boasting of the virtue of his 'blood', is fundamentally inferior to the sane Occidental, not because of the color of his skin, not even because he happens to be in error in his conclusion, but because his *kind* of error shows him altogether at sea with regard to the methods by which conclusions are properly reached and life is reasonably directed.

To the scandal of philosophy, however, after a billion years of animal learning, twenty-five hundred years of science and philosophy, and some three hundred years of deliberate modern empiricism and logical analysis, no one knows quite what is the rationale of the inductive process, why it has worked in the past, and how its working in the past can supply a reason for trusting it now and in time to come. We know, as the savage and Socrates never knew, why 2 × 2 = 4, and why if all men are mortal and all Greeks are men, all Greeks must be mortal. Once granted that we can trust our inductive procedure, we know what is the weight of Sirius, why blue-eyed parents generally have blue-eyed children, what makes meteors — all of them the darkest mysteries to our ancestors, and regarded indeed as intrinsically unknowable. What we don't know is how and why we know those inductive conclusions. This is 'the problem of induction'. To solve it would be to show that all the manifold processes of induction which web together life and science are framed and steeled by logical principles as inexorable as those of mathematical demonstration, and indeed continuous with and deducible from the latter.

The need of induction arises from the fact that whereas with some parts of the world, with some events or states of affairs, we are in direct conscious contact (we perceive them), with other parts we are not — they are out of sight and touch, around the corner, in space or in time or in both, or in some other dimension and direction. Philosophers intricately disagree on just how much world there is altogether, and on just how much can be immediately perceived, but they almost unanimously consent that what we do perceive is at any rate vastly exceeded by what we do not perceive. Not even what we are going to perceive later is perceivable now. Unfortunately, what we do not perceive we nevertheless cannot afford to ignore. Man by nature desires to know, as Aristotle sagely remarked, so that any person worth his salt is agog with divine curiosity concerning what is beyond the horizon of the visible. More urgently, men have a vital practical interest in penetrating the veil. So far is it from being true that what we don't know won't hurt us that the life of a man without knowledge of anything except what immediately strikes his senses would not be worth a moment's purchase.

It was once fabled that some of the indispensable knowledge which goes beyond the immediately perceived was got by a leap of unique insight or by a purely rational contemplation of ideal concepts. Most of it, however, must be got by *inference* from what is perceived. To infer one fact or proposition (the 'conclusion') from another (the 'premise' or 'premises') is to attain a belief in it as a result of believing that the premise is true and logically implies or entails it. If the premise actually does entail the conclusion, the inference is 'valid' or 'cogent'. The conditions under which premises do so entail conclusions are

epitomized in the laws of logic, the science which systematically
describes, among other things, what sorts of propositions entail
each other.

The fundamental pattern of inference by which we know the
unperceived involves a syllogism with a compound premise, or
a conjunction of two premises, one a law, like *All instances of
falling barometer are followed by storms*, and the other a singular
proposition representing a boundary condition or case coming
under the law, like *The barometer is now falling*. The ensuing
conclusion, of course, is *There will be a storm*. On the same
principle we infer that since red-meated watermelons are sweet,
this watermelon, which plugging discloses to be red, will be
sweet. On the same principle, only slightly complicated, the
gunner, apprised of certain laws of ballistics and the characteristics of his munitions, predicts and controls the path of a
projectile, or the astronomer, with data concerning the laws of
motion, plus the behavior of observed bodies, locates an unobserved planet. Pared to its rudiments, the principle may be
formally expressed: Any proposition to the effect that whatever
has a property M (such as being a fat man) has a property P
(such as being good-natured), and that an individual a (say
John McCarthy) has the property M, entails a proposition to
the effect that the individual a has the property P (i.e., that
John McCarthy is good-natured). More shortly, in a formula
almost as old as Aristotle: *All M is P and a is M entails a is P.*[1]

[1] The letters "M", "P", and "a" here are variables, or variable symbols.
I use so few such symbols in this book, and then only in contexts which
explain them so well, that a technical description of their use might confuse
the newcomer as much as it would annoy the initiate. Perhaps we should
remark, however, on a certain variety in the use of the capital letters
"M", "P", "Q", etc. I introduce them above as standing for properties,
like good-naturedness; but it will shortly be convenient to use them also to
stand for classes, like the group or aggregate of good-natured beings. The
property good-naturedness 'determines' the class of good-natured beings.
We can equally say that an individual a 'has' or 'is an instance of' the
property P, or that it is a member of the class P. The phrases "a P" and
"Ps" mean the same, respectively, as "a member of the class P" and
"members of the class P". The form of the proposition *All fat men are*

There is no mystery about this kind of inference, which is the plainest sort of deduction, a syllogism in 'Barbara', traditionally regarded as the perfect mood and figure, here employed with a singular or instantial minor premise, *a is M*, instead of the more usual universal, *All S is M*. Its formula is exactly understood, together with its derivation from the simplest concepts and principles of logic and its extension to the more elaborate instances, like the prediction of a planet's track, where the law involved is a functional equation instead of a mere association of properties, *M* and *P*. Moreover, there is informed agreement on the necessity, not to say triviality, of the principle, and the thorough validity of inferences in accord with it. There may be doubt whether all red-meated melons are sweet, or even whether this melon is red-meated, but no sane man, once he understands the statement, can doubt that *if* all red-meated melons are sweet, and this is one, then this must be sweet. An inference is 'logically valid' in the sense of our present discussion when the statement that if its premise or premises are true, its conclusion is true, possesses this unique kind of internal necessity. The important varieties of such validity are catalogued in logical formulas which may be consulted in any one of a hundred excellent treatises, from Aristotle's *Analytics* to W. V. Quine's *Mathematical Logic*.

Unfortunately for the simplicity of our logic, however, we note immediately that the laws by which we manage our affairs and anticipate unperceived events are less often 'universal', after the pattern required by our previous syllogisms, than 'statistical'. We don't believe that *all* fat men are good-natured, but only that a large proportion are; *most* red-meated watermelons are sweet; falling barometers *generally* portend a storm. Even the scientists of recent years have been informing us that

---

good-natured has traditionally been put "All *M* is *P*", but we can equally say "All *M* are *P*", "All *M*s are *P*", "All *M*s are *P*s". The variations are not elegant but they are customary and sometimes helpful. In the symbolism of recent mathematical logic, *All M is P* is represented as a 'formal implication', $(x) . M(x) \supset P(x)$ — 'For every x, if x is M, it is P'.

most, if not all, of their subtlest generalizations are subject to exceptions. In the cadres of the traditional deductive logic, these modifications make a fatal difference: the propositions that falling barometers generally portend a storm and that the barometer is now falling entail, strangely enough, nothing whatever about an impending storm. *Most M is P and a is M* on the usual schedule is logically as independent of and irrelevant to *a is P* as *Washington was the first American president* is to *The moon has no atmosphere.* Impatient with this finicking of the logician, the native wit of mankind has jauntily transcended the textbook formulas, has found the principle self-evident that if *All M is P* makes it certain that any one *M* will be *P*, then *Nearly all M is P* makes it nearly certain, and has quite satisfactorily predicted its storms and purchased its melons accordingly. This sanguine procedure raises many more delicate theoretical questions than the man of affairs bargains for, but it has been in the main technically vindicated by the development of the logic of probability. The standard and most familiar form of this logic, enshrined in most elementary essays on the subject, adopts the rule of Laplace that a probability is to be equated with 'the ratio of the number of favorable cases to the number of all the possible cases'. This description has been interpreted in several ways, but on one interpretation, almost always assumed in practice whatever theoretical qualms it may occasion, it accommodates our inferences from statistical laws. If there are 750 voters in town, and 600 of them are Republicans, and Sarah Hornblow is one of the voters, there are 600 'cases' favorable to her being a Republican, out of a total of 750 'possible cases'. The probability, in relation to these premises, that she is a Republican is then $\frac{600}{750}$, or $\frac{4}{5}$. The principle of this inference, which may be called "the statistical syllogism" or "the proportional syllogism", is to be formulated thus: If $\frac{m}{n} M$ is *P*, and *a* is *M*, then there is a probability of $\frac{m}{n}$ that *a* is *P*. It extends the scope of deductive validity enormously beyond that of the categorical or universal syllogism and of ordinary mathematical logic.

The principle of the statistical syllogism is not, we shall see, beyond all cavil. Whatever doubts it has provoked, however, are eclipsed by another and much more anxious quandary of the logician who endeavors to found on a bedrock of principle the inferences by which we explore the regions of the unperceived. For even if we grant the validity of both types of syllogistic inference, whence are we to be satisfied of the truth of the premises? The 'minor' premise, to be sure, by which the individual *a* is asserted to be *M*, *The barometer is falling*, for example, is a singular proposition which, when it comes to a showdown, may be supposed directly verifiable by perception — itself a process which deserves inquiry, though of a different sort from the one we are now embarked upon. The 'major' premise, however, the proposition of law, either universal (*All M is P*) or statistical ($\frac{m}{n} M$ *is P*), is a poser. A universal law, to be sure, may be deduced from other such laws, either by an ordinary syllogism with a universal minor premise and a universal conclusion, or by what is sometimes called a 'derivative' or 'demonstrative induction'. The first of these may be exemplified: All who can neither run nor fight must be good-natured; fat men can neither run nor fight; hence fat men must be good-natured. The second is exemplified: The melting point of any pure chemical substance is the same in all specimens; this is a specimen of aluminum bromide and its melting point is 93° C.; all aluminum bromide, therefore, melts at 93° C. These two methods, rife both in science and in common sense, are correct enough, but since they both depend upon premises which themselves are general laws, more general indeed than their conclusions, they only postpone the problem of the origin of our knowledge of any general laws whatever.

The textbooks admit two ways, now, in which laws may be established immediately, by inspection, and with certainty. One of these is the sort of logical analysis of meanings which reveals an analytic truth, a necessary law of logic or an instance of such a law. *All parrots are birds*, for example, and *All Euclidean triangles have the sum of their interior angles equal to two right angles*, are rational or necessary truths amenable to this kind of examination, 'true by definition'. The first is at once evident to anybody who 'gets the idea'; the second is evident after a certain amount of conceptual analysis. The apprehending of such 'essential' or 'verbal' propositions is sometimes called "intuitive induction". Somewhat misleadingly it is described as 'recognizing the universal in the particular': it involves not merely the observation that a given particular is an instance of the universals, *parrot* and *bird* for example, but the observation that they are there necessarily connected as most universals (say *parrot* and *blue*) are not. We shall have more to say later of the scope of such analytic truths, which include the principles of inference themselves, but at best they embrace no more than a minute fraction of the premises needed for our daily affairs or for the natural sciences. Specifically, they include none of the examples introduced on page **6**. Where they are applicable, furthermore, they make the syllogistic form superfluous. It is useless circumlocution to argue that since every parrot is a bird, and Poll is a parrot, Poll must be a bird, when we can as well argue directly that Poll's being a parrot entails, all by itself, that Poll is a bird.

The other mode of directly establishing the truth of general propositions is thoroughly empirical, relying upon commonplace perception of instances of M, and not upon conceptual analysis of the property M in the abstract, and unlike intuitive induction it is competent to guarantee either universal or statistical laws: it is so-called 'perfect induction' or 'summary induction'. This is practicable when and only when we can perceive all the Ms and know that they are all. We can then tick them off singly and conclude, in summary, that all of them, or n per cent of them, or none of them, is P. In this manner, for example, we take a census of Heraldsberg and establish that $\frac{4}{5}$ of its voting population are Republican. Plainly, however, this recourse also, although unexceptionable and indispensable, is closely circumscribed. There aren't many classes which we can survey in this fashion — strictly speaking, unless we arbitrarily limit the class M, we should have to examine everything in the universe to make certain that there is nothing which is M but not P — and no generalization derived by such a survey can ever serve us syllogistically for our inference to the unobserved. I can summarize the Heraldsberg population because it is by definition limited to an explorable area, but when I do I shall have already examined into Sarah Hornblow's politics and shall know whether she is a Republican, so that it will be a base anticlimax to infer at the end that she *probably* is a Republican. That inference may be worth making if I have forgotten the details of my census, and retain merely the statistical summary, but in no case will the method enable us to ascribe the property P to an individual a which has not been already examined with respect to its possession of that property.

The syllogism, in short, whether categorical or statistical, is purely explicative: it enables us to deduce that if a is M it is P only by means of premises which already cover the concurrence of M and P in a. The gap between the perceived and the unperceived, which if it can be bridged at all must be bridged in the establishing of the syllogistic premise, is not bridged when this is established either by intuitive or by summary induction. What we require is an 'ampliative' inference (to use Peirce's phrase), proceeding in accordance with abstract principles whose validity is evident or demonstrable in the same way as the rule of the syllogism, from factual premises attained by summary induction, to something *further*. This ampliative induction is what we usually call simply "induction", and occurs wherever men learn from experience. We believe, for example, that almost all red-hearted melons are sweet because almost all which we have observed or heard about are so. The common man believes that a falling barometer will be followed by a storm because it often has been so in the past. The scientist professes to believe it for a different reason, because it is deducible from more general principles concerning pressure distributions and precipitation points, but these general principles themselves are finally believed because they have been observed to prevail in numerous instances, or for some more complicated inductive reason. In each of these genuine or ampliative inductions we conclude that a certain proportion, say $\frac{m}{n}$, of a class or population M have a property P, from the premise that the property is possessed by that proportion of a subclass or sample, MQ.[2] In practice, the subclass MQ consists of the members of M which have been observed with respect to whether they are P. MQ is then by definition a class whose membership is knowable without our exploring the whole universe, so that the premise that $\frac{m}{n}$ of MQ is P can be established by summary induction. When *all* the observed M is P, $\frac{m}{n} = 1$; when no M is P, $\frac{m}{n} = 0$.

We have before us, then, as concerned in the prediction of the unperceived from the perceived, or in general of one set of facts from another set, three main types of inference: (1a) the categorical syllogism, *Since all M is P and a is M, therefore a is P;* (1b) the statistical syllogism, *Since $\frac{m}{n}$ of M is P and a is M, therefore there is a probability (of $\frac{m}{n}$) that a is P;* and (2) the ampliative induction, *Since $\frac{m}{n}$ of MQ is P, therefore $\frac{m}{n}$ of M is P (probably and approximately).* The coefficient $\frac{m}{n}$ can be any quantity between 0 and 1, inclusive; it is customary, though not imperative, to distinguish between (2a) 'categorical' or 'universal' induction, where it is 0 or 1, and (2b) 'statistical induction', where it is some intermediate value. Each of our specific predictions concerning an individual further event or object, a member of M but not of MQ, may be treated as the fruit of an ampliative induction, (2a) or (2b), in union with a corresponding syllogism, (1a) or (1b). It may also be treated, however, in a foreshortened and condensed manner, as an inference that since $\frac{m}{n}$ of MQ is P, there is a probability of approximately $\frac{m}{n}$ that b, which is M but not MQ, is P. We are more likely to infer, for example, that since most of the wire-haired terriers in our experience have been

---

[2] If M and Q are two properties, say round and red, MQ is their 'conjunction', the property of being both round and red. The *class MQ* is the 'logical product' of the classes M and Q; it consists of that part of the class M whose members are also Q, which is the same as that part of the class Q whose members are also M.

nervously irritable, very probably the terrier now presented for our patronage will be irritable, than to make first an inductive inference about *all* terriers, and then come back syllogistically to this one. The shorter procedure glosses over the main difficulty, however, and since its validity will be assured if and only if we can prove the validity of the more elaborate union of induction and syllogism, we shall find the more gradual way the simpler and more informative.

The three types of inference above would be exemplified, respectively, if (1a) we knew that all the beans in a jar were black and inferred that the first bean we drew would be black; (1b) we knew that $\frac{4}{5}$ were black, and believed that there was a probability of $\frac{4}{5}$ that the one we drew would be black; (2) without knowing beforehand the contents of the jar, we had drawn say 50 beans and finding 40 of them black had inferred that about $\frac{4}{5}$ of all the beans in the jar were black. The foreshortened argument, from particulars to particulars, would run: if we have drawn 50 beans and 40 of them are black, there is a probability of approximately $\frac{4}{5}$ that the next bean will be black. It is stage (2), the genuinely inductive one, which is creative and crucial. Induction is charging the battery of knowledge; deduction is only pressing the switch to light the way with a cognitive energy already stored. 'In the *final* form of a *perfected* science', as Russell says,[3] 'it would seem that everything ought to be deductive'. In that utopian state everything could be deduced from a few fundamental propositions, but those propositions must meantime have been *in*duced. The uses of science, in short, are deductive, but the making of science, and science itself as a living enterprise, is inductive.

Now, we have observed that concerning the first of our inferences above, (1a), no logician would make any demur. Concerning the second, (1b), only a few sophisticated specialists have misgivings. Concerning the third, however, the all-important ampliative induction, whether universal (2a) or

[3] Bertrand Russell, *Our Knowledge of the External World* (London, 1926), p. 43. The italics are mine.

statistical (2b), there is the gravest doubt, denial, and confusion. Unphilosophical men, including scientists, make the 'inductive leap' without a moment's pother. Our inductively grounded conviction that the sun will rise tomorrow, on the premise that it has always risen in the past, is practically indistinguishable in degree from the syllogistic certainty, on the same premise, that it rose last Tuesday. The insurance company charges a premium for John Smith, who belongs to a class of future decedents, at a rate fixed by mortality statistics pertaining to a similar class who have already passed on. So inevitable and indispensable are such inferences that most persons do not notice that they are inferences at all. In the days when philosophers were surer of themselves and their world than today, they assumed without debate that the validity of induction is scribed in the nature of things, and that, with proper precautions, the inference from the observed particulars to the universal law could be demonstratively certain, on all fours with the categorical syllogism or a Euclidean deduction. By the time logicians and epistemologists had exposed the futility of that hope, and shown that the ordinary apparatus of implication makes no provision for such ampliative inferences, the mathematicians of probability were ready with what seemed a proof that the observation of instances can provide at any rate a sound and considerable probability for the inductive conclusion, and most persons, including the scientists, have been content that a probability is all which can justly be required. At the present moment, however, the logic of the probabilists has been almost as badly sapped by criticism as the promises of the dogmatists.

The fate of the methods of empirical science has thus been the reverse of that of the devices of the mathematician and the syllogizer. While the deductive habits of the latter have been proved to everybody's satisfaction, or almost everybody's, in a manner surpassing the fondest dreams of Pythagoras, to be not mere habits, but proceedings in exact conformity with inexorable connections of truths, there has been no increasing consensus in

favor of a logical validity for induction. On the contrary, there
has developed a strong opinion among scientists and philosophers
who have treated the affair, that the inductive inference definitely does *not* have any logical validity analogous to the
standard validity of the categorical syllogism. Some morose
and despairing, some ribald and exultant, they return to the
teaching of David Hume, that although our nervous tissue is
so composed that when we have encountered a succession of
Ms which are P we naturally expect the rest of the Ms to be P,
and although this kind of expectation has often been borne out
by the event in the past, the series of observations never provided a jot of logical reason for the expectation, and the fact
that the inductive habit succeeded in the past is itself only a
gigantic coincidence, giving no reason again for supposing it will
succeed in the future. The carefullest of the inductive methods
of the scientists, in the midst of their most spectacular successes,
are regarded as merely the prevailing conventions of the favorite
soothsayers of our culture circle, and the obligation of the good
citizen to conform by playing the same game has no more logical
warrant than the social imperative to wear a black tie with a
dinner jacket.

The sober amateur who takes the time to follow recent
philosophical discussion will hardly resist the impression that
much of it, in its dread of superstition and dogmatic reaction,
has been oriented purposely toward skepticism: that a conclusion is admired in proportion as it is skeptical; that a jejune
argument for skepticism will be admitted where a scrupulous
defense of knowledge is derided or ignored; that an affirmative
theory is a mere annoyance to be stamped down as quickly as
possible to a normal level of denial and defeat. It is an age
which most admires the man who, as somebody has said, 'has a
difficulty for every solution'. Whether or not this judgment is
fair, however, it is safe to say, with Whitehead, that 'the theory
of induction is the despair of philosophy — and yet all our
activities are based upon it'.[4] So prodigious a theoretical con-

[4] A. N. Whitehead, *Science and the Modern World* (New York, 1926),
p. 35.

tretemps cannot remain a tempest in the professors' teapot. The news that no foundation is discoverable for the procedures of empirical intelligence, and still more the proclaimed discovery that there is no foundation, and still more the complacency which recommends that we reconcile ourselves to the lack, condemn the problem as a 'pseudo-problem', and proceed by irrational faith or pragmatic postulate, will slowly shatter civilized life and thought, to a degree which will make the modernist's loss of confidence in Christian supernaturalism, so often cited as the ultimate in spiritual cataclysms, seem a minor vicissitude. The demand that rational man adjust himself to a somewhat bleaker universe than he once hoped for is only one large and picturesque instance of the sort of re-orientation which inductive intelligence, in its very nature, continually imposes, and well within the proved capacities of human reason and good-will. To dispute the rational validity of induction, however, is to deny that reason and good-will have a purchase on reality, to deny mind's hope of acclimating itself to any world whatever, natural or supernatural.

The word that the house of empirical intelligence is built on a marsh of illogic has already spread outside academic precincts, and has gone far to poison and enervate the lusty confidence with which our Western culture for some centuries was on its way to conquer the world of nature and to discipline the madder human vagaries. For Western culture — any hopeful, humanitarian, knowledgeable, and right culture — depends on induction not merely in its parts, to justify its particular scientific inquiries and political inventions. It depends on induction altogether and in principle. *Spes est una in inductione vera.*[5] It is an inductive civilization, striving always vigorously to strike out the line of that robust and sensitive mean between dogmatism and skepticism, between stiff tradition or intolerance and namby-pamby indifference, which is characteristic of the organon of inductive science. The ruck of our citizens, of course, may still ignore the despair of the logical priesthood and continue

[5] Francis Bacon, *Novum Organum*, aphorism 14 in the first book.

for a long time in the kindly toils of custom, re-enacting in daily affairs the technique of their ancestors though its rationale be vanished. They must inevitably be dispirited thereby, however, being rational animals after all, and the signs of debacle are already visible along an ever widening front.

'Most physicists', laments the philosophical physicist N. R. Campbell,[6] 'have a horror of logic and regard an accusation that their doings conform to logical principles as a personal insult'. They accept their hypotheses by rules of the guild, handed down inarticulately from academic father to son in the laboratory, and are correspondingly undisturbed by the edict of the logicians that their doings after all do not conform to logic. In this innocence their researches also may coast along indefinitely, by rote, like the rhythm of performing elephants. Already, however, scientists pay a certain price for their disdain of abstract principle, in the embarrassing figure they sometimes cut when trapped into pontificating concerning material not regulated by the mores of their profession. Even in their specialties, furthermore, nemesis dogs them, for as physics, biology, or psychology advances, and the relation between hypotheses and evidence becomes more subtle and remote, the sheer mass and quality of evidence becomes less important, and the logical laws of evidence, the more delicate and derivative principles of induction, become much more important. The derivative principles may themselves, to be sure, be worked out almost unconsciously, by simple inductive trial and error, and accepted on animal faith. But the results of so blind a method must be much inferior to a strictly analytic precision, justifying them from first principles of inductive cogency, continuous in turn with the system of mathematics and the syllogism. For what it may be worth, my own judgment, a diffident outsider's, is that the present impasse in physical theory is due mostly to confusions of logical principle.

---

[6] N. R. Campbell and H. Jeffreys, "Symposium: Measurement and Its Importance for Philosophy", *Aristotelian Society Supplementary Volume XVII* (London, 1938), p. 121.

While the disablement of induction plays hob with the pedestrian undertakings of the special sciences, it will do worse with the more delicate and immense topics of metaphysics and morals. On these sciences, where sound induction is most needed and least practiced, devolves the final duty of informing man where he stands and by what route he can attain salvation, in this world or another. They become pointless mummery, and the relativity of ethical judgment becomes irremediable, as soon as we dispute the ultimate validity of argument from the perceived to the unperceived.

More concretely, the implications of inductive skepticism and its eventual effects stretch down into the most intimate projects of common sense and out into the widest reaches of politics, domestic and international. If there is no rational difference between a sound scientific conclusion and the most arrant superstition, there is none between a careful investment and a profligate speculation, between a just and wise decision of a court and a flagrant miscarriage; men are hanged by a process of selection as conventional as eeny-meeny-miney-mo or the human sacrifices of the Aztecs. Indeed, there is no reason on however much theory or experience to turn the steering wheel to follow a curve in the road, or to expect gunpowder to explode, seeds to grow, or food to nourish.

In the political sphere, the haphazard echoes of inductive skepticism which reach the liberal's ear deprive him of any rational right to champion liberalism, and account already as much as anything for the flabbiness of liberal resistance to dogmatic encroachments from the left or the right. The skeptic encourages atavistic rebellion with "Who are we to say?" and puts in theory the forms and methods of democracy on a level with the grossest tyranny. No life at all is possible without the guidance of candid belief, but the trust in democracy peculiarly involves an induction that since it has been satisfactory in the past, it will be satisfactory in the future, and, more than that, the confidence in democracy *is* a confidence in the inductive method in political action. We have trusted men to find right ways of living together by the means of debate and experiment because we trusted what is essentially the scientific method to be logically competent to converge on the political facts of life. The instant this trust is destroyed, the gestures of democracy also become a senseless habit, decelerating like the spin of a flywheel come unkeyed from the driving shaft. Skepticism need not lead directly to cruelty, but it can apologize for a cruel regime, and it provokes a cruel regime because men who believe there is no truth knowable by inductive agreement feel impelled to impose an official myth by methods beyond the pale of criticism or compassion. Political confidence in induction, furthermore, is a far more fragile and theoretical attitude than the inductive confidence of common sense or even of science. Animal necessity and the impact of immediate results will hold us true to inductive method in the homely exigencies of house-keeping, wage-earning, or gun-making; but the profits of inductive reasonableness in morality and politics are diffuse and long delayed, unlikely to keep the habit going when once logical conviction has died. It is unlikely, in short, that a civilization can survive whose characteristic purposes conflict with its fundamental logic and which hence does not *believe* in what it *does*.

To make the matter more pressing, the surrender of the skeptic is in effect no mere refusal and *dolce far niente*. Having spiked the guns of reason, he has invited positive unreason to invade the citadel. All conscious and moral existence is a little clearing in the festering jungle of superstition, whose prowling terrors are fought off only by the courage and confidence of those who know what it is to know. Even within our circle now every doubt which unnerves the defenders of empirical reason is exploited by agents of the enemy, persons who are hostile to reason on principle: the logic haters, mystery lovers, and spell-binders. The obsequies of inductive logic are no sooner austerely announced by the skeptic than they are exultantly celebrated by enthusiasts reveling in the opportunity to advance some extra-scientific dispensation: life, or will, or feeling, imagination or intuition, poetic *Schwärmerei*, pure Reason, revelation, dumb religiosity, authority, ecclesiastical tradition, or tribal animus. The extreme of meticulous incredulity thus joins hands again with utter credulity, and Europe and America, like sick Rome, are ready to fall prey to any quackery.

So much for reflections on the grandeur of our theme. The critical philosopher will remark that they have been rather puffs of our goods and proof of the importance of our business than part of our positive argument. The outlandish disparity between the effects of inductive skepticism and the assumptions of our responsible living and thinking is instructive and it endows any promising theory of inductive knowledge with a *prima facie* claim to sympathy. We must guard, however, against mistaking the evil results of inductive skepticism, actual or eventual, for a proof that it is fallacious or that we have the one right answer to it. Only when induction is already known to be valid, indeed, can any results be validly predicted or described as evil or as good.

This little book contains in outline, I think, the solution of the problem of induction. The problem as here conceived is whether and why a knowledge that in an observed part of a class M the property P is present in a certain proportion gives us a *reason*, analogous to that provided by the premises of a syllogism though less conclusive, for believing that in the whole of the class M the property P is present in a similar proportion, or for believing, if most of the observed Ms are P, that any one unobserved M will have the property P. To the question whether an induction has a logical credibility it returns the answer *Yes*. To the question in what that credibility consists, the answer falls in two parts: an analysis of probability which will reveal that it is a logical credibility relation justly to be described as analogous to strict entailment, though of less degree, and a demonstration that this kind of credibility relation connects, in sufficiently high degree, the premise and conclusion of an induction.

Not to beat around the bush, on the first topic we shall

approve what is pretty nearly the 'classic' theory of probability and the principle of the proportional syllogism: if the fact that all the members of a class have a certain property makes it completely credible that any one given member has it, the fact that most of them have it makes it at any rate very credible (highly probable) that the given member has it. On the second topic, we shall point out how an induction is vindicated by a proportional syllogism of the second level. The inductive problem may be formulated as the problem of showing that it is highly probable that a given sample (MQ) matches in statistical composition its population M, and it is met by showing that the given sample is necessarily a member of a class of possible samples, all of them sets actually included in M, of which the great majority do match statistically the class M. Some readers will need to be persuaded of the truth of this description; to others it will be familiar enough. For all, however, the value of our discussion will consist in maturing and applying the conception in such a way as to make clear that it fills the bill.

The solution is not new or occult. It would be signally incredible if it were. The solution of the problem of induction must be at bottom as banal and monolithic as the process of induction itself. Philosophers and logicians have walked around and over our principle for centuries, sometimes noticing it grudgingly and askance, but never, I think, clearly exposing it or appreciating it in the manner which we shall here attempt. My plan is to present at once the solution itself, in its two parts, observing first what we are asking for when we desire a logical justification of induction, and second how such a justification is forthcoming. When we have the answers to these questions in sharp outline, it will be time to put our conception through its paces and show how it meets the requirements of philosophical theory and of scientific practice and how it avoids the principal species of trouble which infest the subject.

In the nature of the case there must be residual and peripheral questions which our study will raise without settling. This is not a complete theory of knowledge, and we cannot be pledged to deal definitively with the nature of all logical validity nor with the ultimate trustworthiness of any perception of fact. The problem of induction, strictly taken, is the problem how induction may be shown valid on the basis of logic and perception, and not whether logic and perception are valid. At the opposite extreme, again, we evade the duty of detailing particular principles of inductive logic, and still more of giving hints for scientific practice in the application of those principles. Specific laws of evidence, and maxims of procedure, are already current and only wait on the vindication of induction in general to be completed and codified.

2

PROBABILITY

To ask after the validity of induction in general, already for most people the most familiar and convincing kind of inference, is a somewhat peculiar question. What will satisfy us? What do we mean by "validity" here? Until this is clearer, any argument to the point is carrying water in a sieve.

Colloquially speaking, what we want is a proof that the inductive premise makes 'reasonable' our belief in the inductive conclusion. But by "reasonable" we often mean merely *characterized by ordinary sagacity*, and there is no question of the 'reasonableness' of induction in this sense, for an aptitude for induction is just what we mean by "ordinary sagacity". More exactly, however, "reasonable" means *logical* or *according to logic*.

Now, a deductive inference, such as the categorical syllogism, has preëminently this kind of reasonableness. Its conclusion is entailed by its premise or premises: necessarily, if the premise is true, the conclusion is true. Perhaps there are propositions connected by entailments which are not covered by or instances of formal logical laws: the fact that *This is scarlet* entails or necessitates *This is extended* may be anomalous in that way. But the sturdiest and clearest of necessary connections are those which are covered by very formal and general laws of the systematic sort called "logical". The syllogistic inference from *All sailors are superstitious and Johansen is a sailor* to *Johansen*

is superstitious is valid in accordance with the logical law of
Barbara, that a proposition of the form *All M is P and a is M*
entails the corresponding proposition of the form *a is P*. The
non-syllogistic inference from *It is not both raining and blowing*
to *Either it is not raining or it is not blowing* is valid in accordance
with the logical law ('De Morgan's theorem') that any proposition of the form *Not both p and q* entails the corresponding
proposition of the form *Either not-p or not-q*.[1] Such 'logical'
inferences and the entailments on which they are based and the
formal principles of which the entailments are instances have
for many centuries furnished the pattern and *beau ideal* of
reasonableness and validity. We have agreed to take them so,
and it is to them that we now must look to observe more exactly
the nature and source of their authority.

If a logical law of entailment, like the principle of Barbara,
is to furnish a final criterion of reasonable belief it must itself be
known directly and, as it were, infallibly, by sheer contemplation, or else deduced in accordance with laws thus knowable from
laws thus knowable. It cannot, for instance, be an empirical
generalization like *All sailors are superstitious*, which can be
known only by induction, for then the attempt to justify induction by logic would be pitiably circular. That logical principles
can in fact be induced as well as intuited we shall observe later.
That they can, furthermore, be endlessly deduced from one
another, and particularly that the whole system of logic and

[1] In the usual formula, the law is written, "$\vdash: p \mid q . \supset . \sim p \lor \sim q$".
As the capital letters "M", "P", etc., take the place of names of properties
or classes in some of our symbolic diagrams of propositional forms, so the
small letters "p", "q", etc., take the place of whole sentences, standing for
component propositions, in other symbolic diagrams. The marks "$\supset$",
"$\mid$", "$\lor$", and "$\sim$" are merely further abbreviations for the logical con-
nective phrases "If . . ., then . . .", "Not both . . . and . . .", "Either . . .
or . . .", and "Not . . ." ("It is not the case that . . ."). "$\vdash$" is the logical
assertion sign, signifying that any statement of the ensuing form is logically
necessary. We shall never use the abbreviations without verbal translation,
but some readers will appreciate the extra ease and clarity which they
provide.

mathematics can be shown to follow from a few primitive premises containing a few primitive elements or ideas, has been one of the most striking results of modern logical scholarship. The deduction of the principles of deduction is cogent, however, only because every principle by which the deduction takes place, and its every premise and every conclusion, is already intrinsically and self-evidently necessary in its own right. If we ever want to 'prove' a logical principle, this is only when and because a principle which happens to be too complex for our immediate grasp is deducible in accordance with graspable principles from graspable principles.

In just what consists the intrinsic and manifest necessity of a logical principle we have declined to argue. It is a large philosophical problem in itself and affects the validity of induction no more than of mathematical demonstration. We must be content that there is overwhelming agreement, among the veriest skeptics as among the solidest dogmatists, that the principles of logic and mathematics do have a necessity and self-evidence which put them in a category profoundly different from that of even the most reliable propositions of ordinary fact, like *The earth is round* or *Robins lay blue eggs*. Their peculiar truth is unmistakable *a priori*, as soon as the knower opens his mind's eye to their meaning. To this there subscribe with equal complaisance the persons who regard them as 'metaphysical' or 'essential', as 'analytic' or 'tautologous', and as 'verbal' or 'definitional'.

But while we avoid the question of the ultimate philosophic basis of logical necessity, we must observe enough of the content and use of logical principles to understand how they are pertinent to the justification of inference, deductive or inductive, and must guard against some misunderstandings which might seem to disqualify them for our end. Most of the misunderstandings result from certain epithets applied to the principles by technical writers of the skeptical temper who feel that the recognition which they have extended to the peculiar surety of logic must be atoned for by a belittlement of its significance.

Thus the new student of the problem is likely to be instructed that logical principles are only 'laws of thought' or 'laws of language', that they are 'empty', 'trivial', 'tautologous', that being compatible with any possible state of affairs, they say nothing about matters of fact. These are all, I think, unfortunate manners of speaking, but they do not substantially affect our account. Persons who explain that logic is mental or verbal continue to distinguish sharply its principles from ordinary psychological generalizations, like Freud's doctrine of the libido, and from workaday rules of language like the directions for the placing of the verb in dependent clauses in German. They admit, implicitly or explicitly, that logic embodies necessary rules of any possible thought or language which shall discover or delineate the truth about this or any other world. That logical principles are 'empty', 'trivial', 'tautologous', turns out to be just a derogatory restatement of the fact that they are necessary and self-evident. That they are 'compatible with any possible state of affairs' and so do not determine 'matters of fact' is, so far as it affects our purposes, an invidious way of conceding that, being principles of necessity, they do not determine any contingent or non-necessary facts and that they are incompatible, naturally enough, only with the impossible. These strictures do not depart seriously, therefore, from the traditional account, shared by men as diverse as Plato, Leibniz, Hume, and some of the most precisian of contemporary mathematical logicians, that the principles of logic are abstract and analytic truths concerning the necessary traits of the simplest elements of being — quality, relation, instance, negation, number, and so forth.

The occasional statements that logical principles are 'merely hypothetical' or are 'purely abstract', patently false in some injurious senses, are true in some harmless ones. A logical principle, we have already remarked, is certainly not 'hypothetical' in the sense of being a hypothesis needing to be inductively confirmed. In an older sense of the word, a proposition is 'hypothetical' in so far as we consider that *if* it were true, something else would be true, and in another less common one a proposition is 'hypothetical' in so far as we consider that it would be true *if* something else is true. Logical propositions, like any others, can be considered in either of these respects, and we have remarked especially on the systematic connections among logical and mathematical principles by which each implies and is implied by others. This however has nothing to do with the intrinsic truth or cogency of the principles taken singly. The system of logic is not in these respects any different from any other scientific system, say that of physics, and neither the system of logic nor the system of physics is any different from a close-knit fairy story in which, as it happens, none of the propositions is actually true although they rigorously imply one another. The systems of logic and physics are like each other and unlike the fairy story in that not only do their propositions imply one another but each proposition is in fact true. The system of logic finally is unlike that of physics, in a manner signally to its own advantage, in that the truth of its every principle, being necessary, is peculiarly intrinsic and ascertainable without the risk and labor of empirical inquiry. If the fact that every logical principle is related by 'if-thens' or implications to others prevented it from being categorically or unconditionally true in its own right, no proposition whatever could be true, and no proposition could be implied by any other.

There remains one sense, the most common one in logic, in which logical principles are 'hypothetical', namely, that they *contain* if-thens or implications, but this instead of being a disadvantage is exactly the source of their power. The law of Barbara, for example, may be framed: *If* an antecedent and consequent are respectively of the forms *All M is P and a is M* and *a is P*, then *if* the antecedent is true, the consequent is true. The first "if" there represents the great generality of the principle, that it pertains to every situation of the stipulated structure; the second "if" means that the character which it attributes to those situations is itself an implicative or if-then relation. The logical law is not any more removed from the sphere of truth and reality by these *ifs*, of course, than is a law of physical nature — for example, the law of falling bodies, that *if* an object is a freely falling body near the earth's surface, then *if* it has fallen t seconds, its velocity is $32t$ feet per second. The one cardinal difference, again, is that the logical law is necessary and the other is merely contingent.

A logical law is especially ábstract and general, but a very abstract and general law is not one which relates to no concrete affairs but one which relates to extraordinarily many concrete affairs — to every affair, in short, which has the structure stipulated in the formula. It is not merely a mistake, then, but a contradiction, to aver that 'universal propositions about logical forms are propositional functions and as such are in themselves neither true nor false'.[2] A propositional function *is* the form of a proposition, like *All S is P*, which indeed as it stands asserts nothing. A formula of logic, however, just because it is a 'universal proposition *about* logical forms' — for example, that if any proposition of the form *All S is P* is true, then the corresponding proposition of the form *All non-P is non-S* is true — is a full-fledged proposition and is true. Technically, a propositional function contains 'free variables'; in a logical formula, the variables are all 'bound'.

Every logical formula, being an unequivocal statement about situations of a specified sort, already 'applies to the facts' in the important sense that it truly describes the facts. If we are to use the formula in thought and discourse, however, we must 'apply' it in a further sense. We must judge whether a given situation is of the sort to which the given principle pertains. Typically this judgment involves two steps, corresponding to the affirmation of the two "if" clauses in our statement of Barbara above. First, we must recognize whether the presented antecedent and consequent (a possible premise and conclusion), *All sailors are superstitious and Johansen is a sailor* and *Johansen is superstitious*, for example, are actually of the forms *All M is P and a is M* and *a is P*, respectively. If this recognition were

2 John Dewey, *Logic: the Theory of Inquiry* (New York, 1938), p. 157.

indirect or uncertain, the logical principle itself might as well be known only indirectly and uncertainly, for its own lucid necessity would then avail nothing to validate our conclusion. In fact, however, the recognition is certain, direct, and 'analytic' in the same way as our apprehension of the principle. One cannot entertain and understand the logical formula on one hand and the specific propositions on the other without recognizing that the latter are a 'substitution instance' of the former. Indeed, since *If all sailors are superstitious and Johansen is a sailor, then Johansen is superstitious* thus follows self-evidently from the self-evident logical principle, it is all along as self-evidently necessary as the principle is. The principle doesn't 'make' the proposition necessary and the inference valid, nor even 'tell' us that they are so, but is simply the fact that that proposition, and all others of the same form, are necessary. The formula, though it remains necessarily true, is valuable mostly as an aid in classifying and clarifying the infinite variety of such necessary connections.

Once in possession of our specific if-then or implicative proposition, we have in the strict sense 'applied' the logical principle. But in a looser sense, finally, we may still 'apply it' by using the implication to make an inference. We then actually assert the premise, *All sailors are superstitious and Johansen is a sailor*, and draw the conclusion *Johansen is superstitious*. The judgment here involved, that the premise is true, is on quite a different level from the logical judgment that *if* the premise is true, the conclusion must be. It cannot be certified directly by logic, but only, if at all, by logically certifiable implications, deductive and inductive, connecting it with further premises, on back until the proof comes to rest, we may suppose, in premises established by direct perception, without argument, like *This is red and round*. The detail of such grounding, however, is outside our purview now, since we are concerned only with the question, *given* the premises of any one inference, deductive or inductive, what is their connection with the conclusion.

What is the full import, now, of the statement that a logical

principle of implication is a 'credibility' principle, and how is an
entailment, in particular, a credibility relation of the highest
degree? How is it coercive, so to speak, or incumbent on the
believer? "Credible" is Latin for "believable". Strictly, it
should mean what can be or is believed. By a natural transfer
it means what is to be believed or ought to be believed. Clearly
a logical principle of entailment is not physically or psychically
compulsive and does not literally determine what *can* be believed. There is no actual constraint on a person to believe the
principle of Barbara in the abstract, or to infer, given the
premise that all sailors are superstitious and Johansen is a
sailor, that Johansen is superstitious. It would be a better world
than it is if people's minds were fated to work in those ways;
teachers of logic must be content to pronounce that their pupils
ought to believe logical principles, and ought to draw their inferences accordingly. Not even this 'ought', however, can be
part of logic *per se*. In spite of a considerable tradition, logic
itself is not a 'normative' science but a purely descriptive one.
A logical formula does not lay down that a person who believes
a certain kind of premise ought to believe a certain kind of
conclusion, nor even that a person ought to believe that a certain kind of premise entails a certain kind of conclusion. It only
asserts flatly that a certain kind of premise does entail a certain
kind of conclusion, take it or leave it, as chemistry asserts that
hydrogen and oxygen combine to make water. The obligation
to believe logical principles and to infer in accordance with
logical principles is derived indirectly, from the fact that logical
statements are true and that propositions logically inferrible
from true propositions must be true, and that it is *good* that we
should believe what is true. It not only is good in a general way,
redounding to the greater glory of God or to the greatest happiness of the greatest number, but is so advantageous to each
believer singly that every man who knows what is good for him
is committed to believing, so far as he can, in accordance with
logic. A credibility relation, then, is such that when it is known
to hold between propositions p and q, and p is known to be true,

the man who understands what truth is and wants to believe what is true, will be impelled to believe *q*. We accept no responsibility for any other kinds of men — who may keep on believing at random, out of sheer disinterested stupidity, or believing the dictates of pride, self-interest, or childhood association. Even for our kind of man, moreover, the credibility relation has the salutary effects because of its logical character; it does not owe its logical character to its effects.

If now we could demonstrate, using deductive principles in the process, that the premise of an induction entails its conclusion in accordance with one of the systematically collated principles of deductive logic, then we should have solved the problem of induction with supreme éclat. Some men of genius and good sense have hoped for success in such an enterprise, assimilating induction to deduction in a manner like that in which mathematical cogency has been assimilated to logical. Not only, however, has the attempt failed, but the logical profession have demonstrated to the satisfaction of most authorities that such assimilation is impossible. Whereas the assertion of the premise of a valid deduction is strictly *inconsistent* with the denial of its conclusion — the two stand in contradiction to one another — the inductive premise that, say, all the swans in an observed group, no matter how many, have been white, cannot contradict the supposition that other swans are not white, any more than *Mary Smith is a blonde* can contradict *Sarah Jones is a brunette*.

We have cheerfully lowered our sights, accordingly, for a more modest aim. The most, but also the least, which we can ask is to vindicate for induction a validity which is like that of deduction in an essential respect but of less degree — the same in quality, so to speak, but less in quantity. By "an essential respect" I mean that the relation between inductive premise and conclusion must be like the deductive entailment in its logical necessity and objectivity, and with the same capacity for exact formal statement and systematic development, perhaps even in the same terms and from the same first principles, and that it shall be analogously relevant to the truth of the conclusion.

But by "of less degree" I mean that, in spite of these analogies, the relation is less close and conclusive than strict entailment and bequeathes a correspondingly mitigated credibility. Whereas the premise of Barbara makes its conclusion completely credible, or completely warrants a belief in the latter, we are asking after a principle by which a premise can, in the same sense, make a conclusion almost completely credible, or nearly incredible, or more credible than some given third proposition, or credible perhaps to some exactly assignable degree. What we want, in brief, is not a less necessary connection of truth values than demonstrative entailment but an equally necessary lesser connection of them.

These prescriptions, which should take on more definite shape as we try to fill them, have long been approximately and irregularly satisfied by the notion of *probability* as this is formulated by the mathematical theory of probability, sometimes to the tune of rather more contumely than fraternal assistance from the logicians. 'The theory of probabilities' can thus be said to be 'simply the science of logic quantitatively treated'.[3] The task of this chapter, therefore, is to clarify and justify a conception of logical probability in such wise that while accommodating the results of the mathematical theory it shall show probability in an exact and perspicuous way to provide the kind of real credibility which we seek.

It is usual to say that the tradition of deductive logic recognizes only one credibility connection — entailment. Given any two propositions, p and q, then either p entails q, making it 'completely credible', or it does not. Clearly, however, deductive logic has always recognized in the latter case two alternatives: p may neither entail nor preclude q, or it may preclude it,

---

[3] C. S. Peirce, *Collected Papers*, Vol. II (Cambridge, Mass., 1932), p. 392. Peirce continues that its problem is 'to inquire how much the given facts are worth, considered as evidence to prove the possible fact, . . . the general problem of logic'. One may compare Laplace's, "La théorie des probabilités n'est que le bon sens reduit au calcul" (quoted by Jeffreys, *Theory of Probability*, p. 334).

that is, be inconsistent with it, that is, it may entail *not-q*, that *q* is false. If the latter is the case, *q* is made completely *in*credible by *p*. We accordingly have in the scheme of deductive logic definite credibility relations of two degrees, certainty (when *p* entails *q*) and contracertainty (when *p* precludes *q*), a zenith and a nadir separated by the wide zone of irrelevance or independence (when *p* neither entails nor precludes *q*). We took occasion to observe earlier, however, that logical good sense has always been revolted by a scheme which treats alike, as a sheer lack of all logical relation, everything between the antipodes of entailment and inconsistency. The intelligent student, told that strictly *All sailors are superstitious and Johansen is superstitious* does nothing whatever to improve the credibility of *Johansen is a sailor*, is provoked to disdain strict logic; and when in a later trumped-up chapter on hypotheses it is admitted that the monumental findings of science are corroborated by just such arguments, he is confused and impatient. He is distraught again when he observes that while the chapter on the syllogism teaches that unless it is given that *all M is P* or that *no M is P*, the knowledge that *a* is *M* implies nothing concerning whether it is *P*, there are passages in the back of the book which ratify his boyhood assurance that if some intermediate proportion of *M* is *P*, there is at any rate a corresponding 'probability' that *a* is *P*. Again, the textbooks divulge that if we are given in one premise *p-or-q-or-r*, and in another that *p-or-q* is false (i.e., that *p* and *q* are both false), then *r* is certainly true and *not-r* is certainly false; but if the second premise is only that *p* is false, the credibility of *r* is not supposed to be affected at all — although every bookmaker knows, and ordinary exercises in the arithmetic of probability concur, that the scratching of one of three horses in a race notably changes the odds on each of the rest.

We need not interpret these equivocations as the product of a conspiracy by the formal logicians. The logicians are specialists who happen to be concerned with the properties of only the two extreme credibility relations, entailment and preclusion.

They do not deny, if they stay within their rights, that there is
a continuum of credibility relations filling the range between
the extremes, but deny only, correctly enough, that the other
relations are either entailments or preclusions.

If we inspect our above examples of what look like intermediate credibilities, and others which it is easy to think of,
we can rapidly concoct several formulas which make explicit
some promising kinds of intermediate credibilities which in a
more or less exact sense may be said to lie on the logical line
between entailment and preclusion. (1) If a conjunction of
conditions, *p-and-q-and-r* · · ·, taken together entails a consequent *w*, then the realization of any part of the conjunction
favorably affects, other things equal, the credibility of *w*, and
the more conditions are realized, the greater the credibility of *w*.
(2) If a proposition *p* entails a consequent *w*, then, other things
equal, any adjunction that contains *p*, such as *p-or-q-or-r* · · ·,
favorably affects the credibility of *w*, and the fewer the members
of the adjunction, other than *p*, the greater the credibility of *w*.[4]
(3) If *w* entails *p*, that is, if *p* is logically necessary to the occurrence of *w*, then the truth of *p* at any rate affects favorably the
credibility of *w* (and, roughly speaking, the less *w* entails beyond
p, the greater the credibility which *p* lends to *w*). (4) If *p* entails
that one and only one of the *n* propositions, q_1, q_2, · · · q_n, is
true, that is, if it bestows perfect credibility, which we may
measure by the number 1, on the proposition that q_1, q_2, · · · q_n
are exclusive and exhaustive alternatives (that is, just one is
realized in fact), then it bestows on any one member of the set,
say q_i, a credibility of degree $\frac{1}{n}$; and if a conclusion *w* is entailed
by each of *m* members of the set, then *w* has, in relation to *p*,
the credibility $\frac{m}{n}$. If, for example, the conditions of a race (*p*)

---

[4] *Either it is raining or it is blowing* is the 'adjunction' of *It is raining*
and *It is blowing*. Logicians have sometimes called this connection, sym-
bolized by the wedge "∨", "disjunction", but since that word has several
other logical meanings, all much more appropriate, I avoid it. "Adjunction" also has had another meaning in some recent logical writings, but one
which is easily dispensable.

entail that just one of six horses must win (q_1, q_2, $\cdots$ q_6), and if there is no other relevant information, then the credibility of any one horse's winning is $\frac{1}{6}$; and if it is given further that just three of the horses are bays, the credibility that the winner will be a bay is $\frac{3}{6}$ or $\frac{1}{2}$. (5) If a proportion $\frac{m}{n}$ of a class M have a property P, and an individual a is a member of M, *a is P* has a credibility of $\frac{m}{n}$. Given, for example, that three-fourths of the men in a military detachment are Masons, and one member is chosen by lot for special duty, there is a credibility of $\frac{3}{4}$ for the proposition that he is a Mason.

Of these formulas, the last two have special advantages, among them that they provide in principle for measuring degrees of credibility, and that the others, which also are fairly obvious to instructed intuition, may with slight amendment be deduced from them, though not conversely. These two, moreover, are also, with some reservations which we need not explore, equivalent to one another. No. 5 entails No. 4 because we can treat the alternatives q_1, q_2, etc., as composing a class M with n members, of which the true proposition is one member, and m of which have the property of implying w. No. 4 entails No. 5 because the proposition that the individual a is M, M being a class of n members, of which m are P, is tantamount to the assertion that a is identical with one and only one of a set of n individuals and that its identification with any one of m of these individuals implies that it is P.

To make still plainer the rationale of No. 4, let us symbolize the form of the statement that of q_1, q_2, etc., just one is true, by the convention "$\ast$ (q_1, q_2, $\cdots$ q_n)", and let us call this form an "alternation". Then we are declaring that if p entails $\ast$ (q_1, q_2, $\cdots$ q_n), and thus gives perfect credibility to the total alternation (that just one out of the six horses will win, for example), it gives a *pro rata* share, that is, an equal share, $\frac{1}{n}$, of that credibility to each of the exhaustive and exclusive members over which it is distributed. It gives to the alternation of any two or more of the members (the proposition that just one of the three bay horses will win, for example), and to anything implied by that alternation, the sum of their respective credibilities ($\frac{1}{6} + \frac{1}{6} + \frac{1}{6}$, in our example). This principle verifies the conviction that as we reduce the number of members of an alternation, that is, as we reduce the number of possibilities, as when horse after horse is retired from a race, we increase the credibility of any one of the rest of the alternatives, until we reach the deductive mood *tollendo ponens* which eliminates all the alternatives but one and bestows the whole of the original certainty on it. Conversely, if we enlarge the number of possibilities, as when more horses are entered for the race, we must spread further the same total credibility and we necessarily decrease its amount per capita (though we can never by this means reduce it to complete impossibility). In terms of Laplace's 'cases', which we noted in Chapter 1, there were in our example 6 possible cases (just one of six horses could win), of which 3 were favorable (3 out of the 6 possible cases involved a bay horse's winning).

The rationale of our version No. 5 is at least as patent as that of No. 4. If, in the syllogistic mood Barbara, the universal affirmative major premise *All M is P*, in conjunction with the singular minor premise *a is M*, bestows the absolute acme of credibility on *a is P*, and if, in Celarent, the universal negative major premise *No M is P*, together with *a is M* again, lends the same conclusion the absolute zero of credibility, what would give it intermediate degrees of credibility? Well, the only difference between the two conditions which yield respectively complete certainty and complete contracertainty resides in the quantity of the major premise, *All* in the first case, *None* in the second. But are there no intermediate quantities? Indisputably there are. Between *All* (100 per cent) and *None* (0 per cent) there are an infinity of fractional proportions, each of them qualified to generate its characteristic degree of credibility, all equally objective and comprising the same general sort of logicalness. In other words, given the proportional major premise, $\frac{m}{n}$ *M is P*, together with *a is M*, then there accrues to the conclusion *a is P* a logical credibility of degree $\frac{m}{n}$.

This last mode of declaring credibilities is already familiar to us as the proportional or statistical syllogism. Henceforth we shall take it as the typical, if not the only, fundamental variety of argument yielding logical credibilities of intermediate degrees, or 'probabilities'. We shall never, except allusively or accidentally, need to mention any other version of 'probability', and in attempting to show that an induction has a high degree of logical credibility, I shall be content if I show that it has the kind and degree of credibility possessed by the conclusion of a proportional syllogism whose major premise provides, say, that 99 per cent of M is P. In the rest of this chapter and the next we shall be mostly occupied with exhibiting the somewhat prosaic figure of the statistical syllogism in the various lights which show up its virtues as the principle of graded credibility. By way of preliminary we may make sure of a certain minimum vocabulary. The 'middle term' of the syllogism, M, mediates between the subject of the conclusion (the 'minor' term, a) and the predicate property (or 'major' term, P). In probability logic the class M is conveniently called 'the reference class'. The premises in which P and a occur, respectively, we are already accustomed to call the 'major' and 'minor' premises. The ratio $\frac{m}{n}$ is the 'composition' or 'complexion' of the reference class M with respect to the predicate P.

If the sense in which the proportional syllogism yields credibilities intermediate between certainty and contracertainty does not stand out boldly enough from our mere comparison of the respective syllogistic forms, insight may be sharpened by looking at the affair from other angles. The complete cogency of the syllogism Barbara may be said to consist in the logical necessity that among *all* propositions of the form *If all M is P, and a is M, then a is P* in which the antecedents (*All M is P, and a is M*) are true, the consequents (*a is P*) are true. The opposite extreme, of perfect 'anticogency', so to speak, consists of the necessity that in *no* proposition of the form *If no M is P, and a is M, then a is P*, in which the antecedent is true, can the consequent be true. The intermediate cogency, then, of the statistical syllogism consists in the more general fact that it is logically necessary that among the propositions which are of the form *If $\frac{m}{n}$ M is P, and a is M, then a is P*, and which have true antecedents, just $\frac{m}{n}$ must have true consequents. This means, first, that if we choose some one specific value for $\frac{m}{n}$, say .75, then among all the propositions, with true antecedents, which are of the form *If 75 per cent of M is P, and a is M, then a is P*, just 75 per cent must have true consequents. It means, second, that if we choose also definite values for *M* and *P*, say *dogs* and *bite*, then among all the propositions of the form *If 75 per cent of dogs bite, and a is a dog, then a bites*, just 75 per cent of those with true antecedents have true consequents. That is, if it is indeed true that 75 per cent of dogs bite, then as we assert the consequent, *a bites*, of dog after dog, Rover, Ponto, Jerry, Skipper, etc., until we have asserted it just once for every dog, then our assertion must be true in just 75 per cent of the cases.

Instead of speaking of the relative frequency with which compound implicative propositions of the various syllogistic forms have true consequents, it may be more persuasive, though of course logically the same, to speak of the relative frequency with which the corresponding *inferences* would be successful — that is, would result in believing true conclusions. The supreme cogency of the demonstrative syllogism, Barbara for instance, then consists in the fact that all possible inferences, with true premises, which are of the form *Since all M is P and a is M, therefore a is P*, must have true conclusions. The utter absurdity at the other end of the scale consists in the fact that no possible inference, with true premises, of the form *Since no M is P, and a is M, therefore a is P*, can have a true conclusion. The intermediate cogency of the proportional syllogism consists inevitably now in the necessary fact that just $\frac{m}{n}$ of the possible inferences, having true premises, which are of the form *Since $\frac{m}{n}$ M is P, and a is M, therefore a is P*, would result in the acceptance of true conclusions. A highly probable inference is a proof, then, as Locke said, 'such as for the most part carries truth with it ',[5] differing therein from an apodeictic inference which *always* carries truth with it.

It is imperative to note that when we speak here of 'inferences' or 'possible inferences' we mean possible *kinds* of inferences in such a sense that two inferences are distinct when and only when they involve different propositions, and then count as distinct 'inferences' even though nobody in fact 'draws' them. There are as many inferences, in this sense, of the form *Since 75 per cent of dogs bite, and a is a dog, therefore a bites*, as there are objects, *a*, of which it can be said, truly or falsely, that they are dogs. In our present terminology, if I infer on Monday that since 75 per cent of dogs bite, and *Jerry* is a dog, therefore Jerry will bite, and then on Friday have occasion to repeat the performance, with the same premises and conclusion, I have not made two 'inferences' but only one. On the other hand, if nobody at all happens to make this particular kind of inference about Jerry it still counts in our present sense as a member of the class of 'inferences', that is, possible inferences, of the form *75 per cent of dogs bite, and a is a dog, etc.*, and also of the form *75 per cent M is P, and a is M, etc.* This point we shall find very important.

There are other very similar ways, sometimes useful, of summing up the intermediate cogency of proportional syllogisms. Rather than speak or think of probabilities in terms of the relative frequency with which implications have true consequents or inferences have true conclusions, we may consider directly the truth frequency in the class of propositions of which a given conclusion is a member, or the truth frequency in the class of possible beliefs or statements addressed to those propositions. The premises that $\frac{3}{4}$ of the marbles in a bag are black, and that

[5] John Locke, *An Essay Concerning Human Understanding*, Bk. IV, chap. xv, sec. 1. This may be compared with Aristotle's "The probable is that which for the most part happens" (*Rhetoric*, i. 2, 1357a; quoted by J. M. Keynes, *A Treatise on Probability*, London, 1929, pp. 80 and 92). C. S. Peirce, who quoted Locke as above (*Collected Papers*, Vol. II, pp. 393 and 436), stated much of what I state here but more that conflicts with it.

the object which I feel between my finger tips is a marble in the bag, assign the proposition *This is black* to a class of propositions, namely, those attributing black one by one to all the marbles in the bag, among which propositions just $\frac{3}{4}$ are true. In general, we may conveniently say, with tacit reservations to be mentioned later, that a proposition q has a probability of $\frac{m}{n}$ in relation to a premise p when and only when p entails that q is a member of a class of propositions whose truth frequency is $\frac{m}{n}$. When we 'draw a conclusion', then, we draw it, so to speak, as if it were a ticket from a bagful of possible conclusions of which our evidence tells us the truth frequency. If the evidence entails the conclusion, all the tickets in the bag are truths; if it precludes it, none of them is a truth; if it gives it a probability of .75, three-fourths of the tickets are truths; and so forth.

The one danger in treating of these topics in terms of 'possible inferences', 'propositions', and the like, is that the terms suggest a mystic departure from the realm of actualities to disembodied possibilities and Platonic hypostatizations. Whether philosophy in general can get along without disembodied possibilities I do not know, but I hasten to point out that our present theory does not need them. Our allusions to 'possibilities' and 'propositions' are only rhetorical conveniences, translatable without residue into statements concerning plain matters of fact. The success frequency in the class of possible inferences whose conclusions are propositions concerning biting dogs, for example, is constituted by the actual statistical ratio of biters among mundane dogs, and our whole treatment of the 'possibilities' can be reformulated without mention of anything more un-earthly and ethereal than the behavior of the flesh-and-blood animals themselves, and the same is true *mutatis mutandis* for other probabilities and reference classes. By keeping in mind that our probabilities are really constituted by the actual statistical distribution in the reference class we shall avoid some logical difficulties connected with the notion of statistical frequencies in classes of *propositions* which arise from the fact that propositions *per se* are not concrete countable objects as dogs are. Taking care never wholly to lose sight of the factual foundations of our probabilities, however, we may safely explain them in any of the locutions which are popular today. Thus we can speak of the event or fact of a certain marble's being red, or the inherence of the property red in the marble, or the truth of the proposition (the logical unit of meaning) *This marble is red* or of the sentence "This marble is red" or even of the 'idea' or 'belief' that this marble is red. At all these levels we shall have corresponding classes with parallel frequencies, and any of these modes of expression will issue in the same estimate of credibility.

The special devotion of science, common sense, and the logic books to universal laws, *All S is P*, creates the impression that such laws have a firmer place in reality than the merely proportional ones on which probabilities depend, and that our intermediate credibilities must therefore have a kind of accidental and irregular status. Nothing could be further from the truth. Any two properties must be connected by some law, universal or merely proportional. No matter what M and P may be, round and blue, man and mortal, armadillo and ultramontane, either all M is P, or no M is P, or some intermediate proportion of M is P. But it is vastly more common for some intermediate proportion of M to be P than for all M to be P. Such connections are not literary or accidental; they are native and ubiquitous, bedded deep in the total matrix of world facts. I am not much interested in what proportion of round things are blue, for example, because I suspect it is about the same as the proportion of things in general which are blue, so that the information that a moot object is round does not affect whatever probability I previously ascribed to its being blue. Nevertheless indubitably, in the nature of things, some one proportion — it may be 23.456 per cent — of the round things in the world at large, or on earth, or on earth in this century, are blue. Our minds at any moment are simmering with countless more or less indefinite and inaccurate estimates of such proportions, and we choose our beliefs and lay our bets and guide our lives on the corresponding credibilities. The fact that we seldom know the exact fraction $\frac{m}{n}$ is no derogation from the logical rigor of our estimates, but only from their determinateness. The corresponding credibilities, described indefinitely or 'topologically', as 'nearly sure', 'barely likely', 'more probable than so-and-so', are no less objectively logical and necessary than the preciser degrees.

Our standard account of probability, if it be admitted, settles in principle and in the affirmative the question whether anything reputedly so intangible as credibility can be measured. The kind of measurement generally admired as the most satisfactory is that of spatial extension, length, because of its ready conformity to neat and easy arithmetical rules. Thus we can readily mark off equal lengths on a yardstick, for example, while conversely if we stick together two lengths end to end we have a length whose measure is the sum of the measures of the lengths separately. Time and weight are hardly less nicely measurable. At the opposite extreme, however, goodness, happiness, and various other flavorsome characters are often said not to be measurable at all. Credibility, some have expected, must belong in the latter category. Because credibility however is a logical and even an arithmetical character, and not at all 'spiritual', the contrary is the case. If the quantity we assign to a probability is indefinite, the fault is our own inadvertence.[6] It is always in principle possible to establish for our credibility a measure even more unequivocal than that of extension. What determines the credibility is the ratio of the numbers of objective classes, ascertainable by the one kind of measurement whose ease and exactness surpass those of length, namely, sheer *counting*, a process which depends on no factitious units, like the meter unit of length, but only on the discrimination of individuals univocally identified by the properties M and P.

In the preceding discussion of the derivation of credibilities from statistical proportions, I have written generally as though

[6] This and the following sentence we shall find must be qualified, from another direction, with regard to inductive probabilities.

all the classes with which we are concerned were finite. This is indeed virtually the case — virtually, that is, for our present purpose. So long as we are concerned with finite classes, probabilities of 0 and 1 are equivalent to deductive preclusion and entailment, respectively. When the 'reference class' M is infinite, however, this equivalence does not quite obtain. For "No M is P" does not mean merely that the *proportion* of M which is P is 0, but that the *number* of M which is P is 0, and "All M is P" does not mean merely that the proportion of M which is P is 1, but that the number of M which is not P is 0. When the number of M is finite, the two formulations are equivalent, but not otherwise. When M is infinite, then *No M is P* entails that the proportion of M which is P is 0, but *The proportion of M which is P is 0* does not then entail *No M is P* because if the number of M is infinite, the number of Ms which are P might be any finite number and the proportion of M which is P would (by a common arithmetical rule) still be 0. More fundamentally, again, the admission of infinite reference classes defeats our account by ruling out any definite proportion of Ps among the Ms. Mathematically, if both the number of M and the number of MP (the class of things which are both M and P) are infinite, there is no determinate ratio between them, and so no definite credibility that a given M is MP. The lavish allusions to infinite populations in the recent literature of probability have had to evade this difficulty by the concept of the limit — if M is an *ordered* class, such as a series of events on successive dates, the proportion of MPs within it can be equated with the fraction on which the proportion converges, if it does converge, as we take longer and longer sections of the series, that is, the fraction about which the proportion fluctuates more and more narrowly as the series is extended. Actually, however, we can scout such precautions because we never or almost never deal, in science or in common sense, with classes which are literally infinite. We shall continue, therefore, to count *All M is P* and *100 per cent M is P* as equivalent, and *No M is P* and *0 per cent M is P* likewise, and to count probabilities of 1 and 0 as equivalent, therefore, to entailment and inconsistency respectively.

Every object, say a, belongs to a great number of classes besides the one M on which we have imagined ourselves concentrating. Every inference correspondingly belongs to a great number of different classes of inferences: the inferences determined by the membership of M, the inferences actually made by a given person, and so forth. Each of these classes of inferences has its success frequency which, if it were known, would yield a corresponding credibility to the conclusion. In our examples the class of inferences is determined by the class M because M is assumed to be the only class of which we know both (1) that a is a member of it, and (2) what its composition is.

Here we touch on the characteristic of probabilities which, though it is bound up intrinsically with the very concept of graded credibility, is at once most peculiar and most difficult for the new student of the subject to understand and appreciate: namely, its 'relativity'. Logical credibility of whatever sort, probable or apodeictic, is 'relative' in the sense that it is a *relation* between antecedent and consequent, or premise and conclusion. A proposition q cannot be 'probable' all by itself, or 'entailed' all by itself, but is probable in relation to, or 'on', another proposition p, or is entailed *by* it, etc., as the case may be. Probability is further 'relative' in the sense that it occurs in innumerable different amounts or degrees, and the same proposition q may have one degree of credibility in relation to one proposition, have innumerable others to other propositions, and be entailed by and inconsistent with still other propositions. What we call 'the' credibility or 'the' probability of a proposition is its credibility or probability in relation to the propositions which we happen, at the moment the statement is made, to know to be true, somewhat as when we speak of 'the vicinity' we refer to what happens to be near us at the time of speaking. When a proposition is entailed by what is known to be true we call it simply 'certain'; if it is inconsistent with what is known, we call it 'certainly false' or 'contracertain'. If it has a probability of $\frac{m}{n}$ in relation to what is known, we say that 'the probability' of the proposition is $\frac{m}{n}$. It is important to notice again that none of this means that there is anything 'subjective' or 'dependent on our state of mind' about any credibility relation, probable or apodeictic. The credibility relations hold objectively and absolutely; the state of our knowledge does not affect them but only determines which of them is for us at present 'the' pertinent one. This is no more mysterious than the fact that George may be at the same time really taller than Mary and shorter than Harry, and that when Harry says "*I* am taller than George" he is right but when Mary says "*I* am taller than George" she is wrong.

There is still, however, a significant difference between the end points of the scale of credibilities and the middle reaches. The apodeictic extremes of credibility preserve a special sort of absoluteness: once given the truth of the current premises, whatever is entailed by them is forever certain, and whatever is inconsistent with them is forever contracertain. No additional knowledge can ever make 'the' credibility of them any different. For this reason demonstrative principles and their corresponding inferences have an extreme simplicity. Intermediate credibilities or probabilities, on the other hand, are stubbornly 'relative' in a further respect. They are by their nature inconclusive, not merely in the sense that they *are* intermediate, but also in the sense that so long as 'the' credibility of a proposition is thus intermediate, it may be superseded by the establishment of new premises determining a new net credibility, greater or less than it. Thus, for example, the net current probability that an approaching hurricane will strike Manchester, N.H., fluctuates as new data are broadcast by the weather bureau. Given *only*, again, that there are seven horses entered in a certain race, 'the' probability that any stipulated one of them, say High Tension, will win, is on our principles $\frac{1}{7}$, but in practice an interested habitué will normally have further information, derived perhaps by induction from past experience of the several horses, or horses similar to them, and for him 'the' probability may be

very different (though it need not be). When the probability of
a conclusion r in relation to the combined evidence pq differs
from its probability in relation to part of the evidence, p, then
the new evidence q is said to be 'relevant' to r with respect to p.

It follows from all this that any general logical statement of
the degree of credibility acquired by a given kind of conclusion
from a given kind of premise can be only a statement of its
credibility in relation to that premise alone, uncomplemented
by any relevant further information: given *only* that $\frac{m}{n}$ M is P
and a is M, there is a probability of $\frac{m}{n}$ that a is P. No such precaution is needed for a demonstrative principle: if q is entailed
by p, or is inconsistent with p, it is entailed by or inconsistent
with any conjunction of propositions in which p is included.

A careful understanding of this essential trait of graded
credibilities not only will obviate certain easy objections to our
elementary rules of probability measurement but will sub-
stantiate our philosophy by showing how intermediate probabilities must be coördinate with entailment rather than subordinate to it. For there is a temptation to maintain that when
p bequeathes to q a probability $\frac{m}{n}$, there is not a relation analogous to entailment, albeit of an intermediate degree $\frac{m}{n}$, holding
from p to q, but only a strict relation of entailment holding from
p to the secondary proposition $q\text{-}has\text{-}the\text{-}probability\text{-}\frac{m}{n}$; or at any
rate that one way of putting it is as correct as the other. But in
fact, although it is often convenient to speak in accord with this
interpretation, and we easily fall into saying "The evidence
implies that the jury's decision has a high probability" or "It
entails a high probability for it", instead of "implies it with a
high probability", the interpretation, taken literally, is quite
impossible because of the logical law aforementioned, that whatever is *entailed by* p must be entailed also by the conjunction of
p with any other proposition, say by pr, and this is emphatically
not true of such a consequent as $q\text{-}has\text{-}the\text{-}probability\text{-}\frac{m}{n}$. It
follows, rather oddly, that although a true proposition of the
form q *has the probability* $\frac{m}{n}$ *in relation to* p is analytic and necessary, like a statement of entailment, and its denial is self-

contradictory, *p is true but q does not have the probability* $\frac{m}{n}$ is not self-contradictory.

By describing probability in terms of truth frequencies and also as a kind of relation which has different values for different relata, we have conquered once for all, I should think, the temptation to regard a probability as a degree of *truth*, as though some propositions hung by nature in a limbo of mere probability, somewhere between complete truth and thorough falsity. Every proposition is unqualifiedly true or unqualifiedly false. Its probabilities subsist in another dimension, not in the range between truth and falsity but between entailment and preclusion. The best earnest that a probability cannot be a kind of intermediate truth value is that we define "probability" by reference to truth. To say that a proposition has a probability of .75 is not to say that it is three-fourths true, or true in the degree .75; it is to say that it is one of a definitely identified class of propositions among which 75 out of 100 are unqualifiedly true and 25 flatly false.

It is not necessary for us to contend that the proportional syllogism provides a complete theory of probability, or a whole definition of "probability", but only that it does clearly embody a probability relation which is a degree of implicative connection intermediate between strict entailment and inconsistency, and that whatever else the ultimate analysis of probability may bring forth, it must justify at least the proportional syllogism. The fact is that the proportional syllogism may not be capable by itself of accommodating all the forms of probability inference which are scientifically important and which the best regarded authorities as well as enlightened intuition have customarily approved. Although the proportional syllogism is all that we shall need in the vindication of induction, therefore, it may need some supplement if it is to vindicate, in turn, some of the most valuable uses of the results of induction. One such supplement, if not the only one, may be a provision for a stronger form of the classic multiplicative law of probability than the proportional syllogism yields by itself. The multiplicative law, which is perhaps the most often used of the rules of the ordinary probability calculus, and is required for the derivation of very important further rules, is the law that the probability of a conjunction of two propositions, *q and r*, in relation to any evidence *p*, is equal to the product of the probability of *q* in relation to *p*, times the probability of *r* in relation to the conjunction *p and q;* or, what comes to the same thing, it is equal to the product of the probability of *r* in relation to *p*, times the probability of *q* in relation to *p and r*. The law is more familiar in the briefer and less exact phraseology, "The probability that both of two events will occur is equal to the probability of the one multiplied by the probability of the other as affected by the occurrence of the first". Symbolically, writing "*qr/p*" to mean *the probability of q-and-r in relation to p*, and so forth, it runs:

(1) $\vdash: qr/p = q/p \times r/pq = r/p \times q/pr.$

In some situations this follows without bother from the proportional syllogism and the rules of arithmetic alone. If there are 100 dogs in the neighborhood, for example, and we know that 75 of them will bite, we can calculate that the probability that a given one of the neighborhood dogs, Skipper, will bite is $\frac{75}{100}$, while the probability that another dog, Gabriel, is a biter too if Skipper is one of the biters is $\frac{74}{99}$ (with Skipper accounted for there are only 74 biters left, and only 99 dogs). The probability that they are both biters is accordingly $\frac{75}{100} \times \frac{74}{99}$, or $\frac{5550}{9900}$. This, however, is exactly the result yielded by a single proportional syllogism to the effect that there are 100 × 99, or 9900, *pairs* of dogs in the neighborhood, and that of these pairs 75 × 74, or 5550, contain two biters each, so that since Skipper and Gabriel are one of the pairs, the probability that they are a pair of biters is $\frac{5550}{9900}$. Suppose, however, that you meet a neighborhood dog on your way home and I meet one too, and we do not even know whether it is the same dog. The probability that the dog I meet is a biter is .75; the probability that the dog you meet is a biter is also .75. The multiplicative law gives us a probability of $\frac{75}{100} \times \frac{75}{100}$, or $\frac{5625}{10000}$, that we have both met biters. Unlike the previous result, however, this cannot be easily derived directly by a proportional syllogism concerning pairs of dogs. There seems to be in the situation no actual class with a composition of .5625 with respect to biting, yet our logical wit tells us that it would be absurd to admit the multiplicative probability in the one instance and reject it in the other. We might be able to dispose of this and some other anomalies associated with the multiplicative law by calculating in terms of compound 'cases', pairs consisting each of one man (you or me) and one neighborhood dog. Without arguing for or against this proposal, I shall assume hereinafter the general validity of the multiplicative law. If need be, then, I would expand our description of probability to at least this extent: to say that a proposition q in relation to data p has a probability $\frac{m}{n}$ is to say that *either* p and q are the antecedent and consequent respectively of a statistical syllogism involving the composition $\frac{m}{n}$, *or* p provides for two or more statistical syllogisms whose combined effect in accordance with the multiplicative rule (or other rules if we admit them) is to yield a probability $\frac{m}{n}$ for the proposition q. Let me emphasize, however, that I do not believe that the multiplicative rule really requires such a dispensation, and that we anyhow do not need the rule to justify induction.

Similar provision might have to be made for the classic additive law: the probability of an adjunction of two propositions, *Either q or r*, in relation to any evidence p, is equal to the sum of their separate probabilities on that evidence, less the probability of their conjunction. Colloquially, 'the probability that one or the other of two events will occur is equal to the sum of the probabilities of the events separately, less the probability that both will occur'. Symbolically, writing "$q \vee r$" for *Either q or r:*

$$(2) \quad \vdash : q \vee r/p = q/p + r/p - qr/p.$$

This law too is unneeded for our main preoccupation, the validation of inductive inference, but in several connections to come it will be convenient to be able to refer to both laws.

3

THE MATURITY OF THE CHANCES

There is both embarrassment and encouragement in the fact that our account of graded credibilities has turned out to be nearly or quite equivalent to what is often called 'the classical theory of probability'. There is encouragement because the classical theory is so firmly rooted in common sense and has been so thoroughly explained and applied in some centuries of mathematical, scientific, and philosophical literature that any really contrary account would be handicapped by an almost insuperable burden of proof. There is embarrassment on the other hand because the prevalence of the classical philosophy of probability has raised up typical bugbears in its despite. Our traditional doctrine falls heir consequently to traditional doubts and reproaches and must eventually come to terms with rival theories.

One kind of reproach and rival we need not fear to face, viz., the kind which declares that there are more varieties and sources of probabilities than the proportional syllogism or the reckoning of 'cases' accounts for. The logical intuitionism of the Cambridge school, for example — Johnson, Jeffreys, Keynes, Whitehead — which has dominated much English and American writing on the subject, agrees explicitly with our theme that probability is the same kind of propositional connection as entailment and inconsistency though of intermediate degrees. It diverges from our classical account by arguing that probability is ultimately an unanalyzable character to be acknowledged by a rational intuition and hence not only cannot be resolved into arithmetical ratios or proportions but is discoverable in many circumstances where no such ratios or proportions are given. Although the Cambridge school are logical atomists, their unanalytic and non-numerical variety of the notion of 'logical proximity' has an obvious affinity with the neo-Hegelian doctrine of Bosanquet, for example, which finds in syllogistic necessity only a high degree of that organic harmony which is directly intuited in lower degrees in less conclusive inferences. These expansive theories, however, need not deny anything which we assert or anything which we require for vindicating induction; they only assert more than we require. The Cambridge school do 'analyze' their probabilities to the extent of developing for them rules which turn out to be none other than the rules of the classic calculus founded upon 'cases', and their intuitions seem generally, though not always, satisfied of the validity of the proportional syllogism. I will not forbear remarking, none the less, in spite of a long prejudice in their favor, that the non-numerical theories of probability not only are undesirably mystical, but, while asserting more than we require to validate induction, assert more than is true. Their authors have not been able to make out a very impressive case for non-statistical probabilities nor to give us important and plausible examples. I grant that there are many inferences in sound thought and discourse, supporting common-sense convictions or scientific and philosophical hypotheses, which do not at first sight appear to be grounded in relative frequencies, and I grant that these are not to be denied the title "probable", but I think that all of them on closer inspection will prove, in some vague, roundabout, or approximate way, to depend upon relative frequencies after all.

For similar reasons we need not be disconcerted by sundry other theories of logical probability which promise like ours to provide a measure for that character but propose a kind of measure different from the statistical syllogism. Adopting from

the Cambridge school the concept of *logische Nähe*, the Viennese
Wittgenstein and Waismann worked out more explicitly the
principles on which, in relation to evidence p, 'the numerical
probability of a proposition q will be the greater, the less what
is asserted in q exceeds what is already contained in p'.[1] To
measure such excess the authors borrowed or devised the doctrine of the '*Spielraum*'. This philosophy, somewhat oddly and
variously expressed by its several supporters, may be roughly
described as assigning to a consequent q in relation to an antecedent p a probability equal to the ratio between the number of
possible states of the universe which are compatible with the
conjunction of the antecedent and consequent, pq, (the 'leeway'
which they leave, so to speak) and the number of possible states
which are compatible with the antecedent p. The results of this
rather forbidding principle, so far as its authors have been able
to apply it, appear to be virtually the same as those of our classic
formula for favorable and possible cases.

The notion of logical proximity is differently utilized by other
writers, with and without a formal metric. William James, for
example, held that a proposition is to be called probable in so
far as the requisite conditions for its truth are known to be
present or 'few hindering conditions are in sight',[2] and C. J.
Ducasse has proposed a more finished version of a similar idea.[3]
These suggest a new dimension of probability, the dimension
connoted by "$\tau\grave{o}$ $\epsilon\grave{\iota}\kappa\acute{o}s$", "verisimilitude", "likelihood", and
"*Wahrscheinlichkeit*". Whereas our classic doctrine of cases

[1] This description of the theory's purpose is quoted from Karl Popper,
Die Logik der Forschung (Wien, 1935), p. 97, though Popper does not
approve it. In translating I have taken the liberty of interchanging "p"
and "q" to conform to our own custom. A uniquely concise survey of
theories and problems of probability, weighted somewhat in favor of
skepticism and statistics, is Ernest Nagel's *Principles of the Theory of
Probability* (Vol. I, No. 6, of the *International Encyclopedia of Unified
Science*, Chicago, 1939).

[2] *Some Problems of Philosophy* (New York, 1911), pp. 225–226.

[3] See "A Neglected Meaning of Probability", *Proceedings of the Sixth
International Congress of Philosophy* (New York, 1927), pp. 343–347.

may be paraphrased as describing the probable as what is *usually* true, this concept would have us describe it as what is *like* the truth, 'in itself, in its evidence, in some more or fewer of its circumstances'.[4] The new dimension, which we may call "analogy", we may grant deserves more attention than we have here given it. Meantime, however, no adequate account of it is available, and there is every reason to believe that it will not prove to be the sole or even an independent principle of credibility. Everyone who has entertained it has admitted also I think the credibilities engendered by statistical ratios. James, for example, added that when the conditions are too numerous or confused 'we treat a thing as probable in proportion to the *frequency* with which things of that *kind* occur', and Aristotle, Locke, and Butler passed from the one idea to the other with even less ceremony.

Much more drastic in their effect on our argument, if we should concede them, are theories which, instead of admitting more logical credibilities than are provided by such statistical syllogisms as we have been employing, do not admit even so much. Of these there are two main varieties, the so-called 'frequency' theory and the 'subjective' theory of probability.

Under the name "frequency theory" there is sometimes defended a commonsensical idea that 'the probability of an event' is 'dependent on the frequency with which the event has happened in the past'.[5] In these terms the probability that there will be a storm, for example, given that the barometer is falling, is furnished by the relative frequency with which, up to now, falling barometers have presaged storms. This is good sense, of course, and is in some degree and for some circumstances justified by any logical validation of induction. Taken tech-

[4] Joseph Butler, *The Analogy of Religion*, Introduction, § 3.
[5] R. H. Nisbet, "The Foundations of Probability", *Mind*, Vol. xxxv (1926), p. 1. If Hume admitted what he would call a 'philosophical' kind of 'the probability of causes' in distinction from 'natural' probability and the 'probability of chances', this is it. It is apparently the gist of the 'frequency theory' defended by Morris Cohen, *A Preface to Logic* (New York, 1945).

nically, however, as the first principle of probability, it superbly
repudiates the inductive problem by erecting the foreshortened
kind of induction from particulars to particulars into the very
definition of the subject, and so asserting the validity of induction by the precarious right of an ultimate postulate or intuition.
The intuition is implausibly *ad hoc*, it provides no clear connection between inductive and deductive validity, and in its
pristine form it entails such anomalies as that if I have seen just
three crows and they were all black, then it is *certain* not only
that my next crow will be black but that all the crows I shall
ever see will be black. To avoid the last result, the theory may
be amended that the probability thus provided is only more or
less *reliable*, according to the number of the observed instances.
The reliability of a probability here required, however, turns
out to be nothing other than what we have been calling "the
probability of a frequency" — that is, it is the inductive credibility of the hypothesis that the series in question will maintain
the statistical composition apparent in its observed stretches.
If such a reliability is not to be justified by a method like ours,
founded in the one systematic theory of probability, its acceptance must remain a primitive fiat or animal faith. In the latter
event the doctrine merges with the usual version of the frequency
theory.

The 'frequency theory', in the common acceptation of the
term, is best described as a theory of 'deductive' probabilities
which is like ours in admitting the statistical syllogism and
requiring that the moot object or event *a* shall be a member of
the reference class *M* whose composition determines the probability, but unlike ours in demanding that the reference class be
of a very special sort, an infinite series of 'trials' or 'observations' (or 'inferences') with the predicate property *P* distributed
at random within it, and hence that the composition $\frac{m}{n}$ shall be
not the actual ratio of the number of *MP* to the number of *M* but
the limit on which that ratio converges as the series is prolonged.
Thus a frequency theorist would refuse to admit that the probability of drawing a red card from a pack can be furnished by the

proportion of red cards in the pack but would hold that it must consist in the limit of the relative frequency with which red cards are obtained in an infinite series of drawings (with replacement after each drawing). This theory is generally unprepossessing as an account of probability because of its artificiality and narrow scope, but it is hopeless as a foundation for a theory of induction because the composition of such endless series, if knowable at all, would have to be known by induction, with a 'reliability' which the theory itself cannot account for. The frequency theory of *probability*, in contrast with the mathematically similar method of handling the statistics of mass phenomena which sometimes is called by the same name, has few adherents today, and might have still fewer if there were not a continuing confusion between the very different purposes of the logical theory of credibility and the statistical theory of random series.[6]

Whereas the frequency theory of probability avers that there are logically cogent probability relations (or approximations thereto) but has to admit that none is knowable unless we can presuppose an independent principle of induction, there are subjective theories of probability which deny that there is even in principle any such thing as logically cogent implication of intermediate degree. What have been called "probabilities" in this connection, the theories run, are no more than *de facto* tendencies to believe, resultants of the psychological allure of the respective propositions and the susceptibility of the person who contemplates them. Probability was thus for Hume, at least in its primary capacity as a 'natural' relation, and later for De Morgan, only degree of belief. For others (for Bayes and Ramsey, for example) it has consisted of one's willingness to risk a measurable loss on the chance of a measurable gain. Some adherents to the frequency theory (Bridgman and Mises,

[6] This, I take it, is the upshot of the "Symposium on Probability", by Bergmann, Carnap, Kaufmann, Margenau, Mises, Nagel, Reichenbach, and Williams, *Philosophy and Phenomenological Research*, Vol. V (1945), pp. 449–532, and Vol. VI (1945), pp. 11–86.

for example) and to the *Spielraum* theory (Waismann, for example) have held that beyond the very limited area with which their theories can cope, what is called "probability" is no more than a state of mind or a degree of semantic convenience. The upholders of such opinions are clear enough that these degrees of belief, or propensities to wager, are influenced by a knowledge of objective frequencies or ratios of cases, but hold that the probability is in the last analysis constituted by the psychological attitude and not by the objective frequencies. A probability is thus a 'credibility' in the literal sense, an ability-to-be-believed, and not in the logical sense, an objective warrant for belief. This doctrine is a flat denial of ours, but conversely is refuted, I think, by our whole defense of the concept of intermediate logical credibilities. Significantly, perhaps, nobody actually believes the subjective theory in any other sense than that he will state it when under the prod of epistemological debate. Its authors never actually hold, as their theory requires, that a person can improve his chances at a card game by drinking himself into an optimistic frame of mind. On the contrary, they use the objective calculus of probabilities as scrupulously as anybody and praise and condemn people's conclusions, not in accordance with the sheer fervor with which they are held, but in accordance with their conformity to the rules of evidence.

If our description of probability need not be much afraid of competition from other professional philosophies, it certainly is congenial enough with the ideas and actions of the ordinarily shrewd citizen. The statistical syllogism is so much a part of the mental furniture of the common man, the scientist, and the philosopher, that our principal risk in defending it is that our labors only dim a natural light already as lucent as any justification could be. The intuitive validity of the statistical syllogism is witnessed obviously by our unhesitating readiness to lay bets and plan business on a basis of relative frequencies, known or estimated. It is witnessed more subtly and perhaps more profoundly by the equally ready converse use of it as a scheme of explanation. Just as we should usually be content that the fact that a falling body has hit the ground at a velocity of 64 feet per second is explained by the propositions that it has fallen for two seconds and that all bodies near the earth's surface accelerate 32 feet per second per second, so we should be only a little less content with the explanation that a given cat is deaf because it is an albino and *most* albino cats are deaf.[7]

The intuitive popularity of the statistical syllogism we have not left to stand alone but have analytically approved by noticing just how the statistical syllogism is cognate with the irreproachable categorical syllogism. We can hardly go on to apply our analysis to the validation of induction, however, without taking the precaution of disarming first some of the objections which the honest inquirer is on second thoughts most likely to feel toward our doctrine. To what extent exactly have we met the requirements laid down for a theory of graded credibility at the beginning of the previous chapter? Just two puzzles I think are important enough to be specially disposed of: doubts concerning 'the maturity of the chances' and doubts concerning 'randomness'. These we must allay in context in that order.

At this fundamental level where we have examined the nature of credibility itself, we can perhaps less fairly speak of 'demonstrating' that the statistical syllogism provides genuinely intermediate degrees of logical credibility than of assisting ourselves to discern that such is the case. Any doubts which haunt us are correspondingly difficult to put a finger on and must be laid by patient re-thinking and self-searching, asking of any among us who still is not satisfied with our achievement what he misses in it.

None can well dispute that on the strictly logical side we have made out a deep analogy between our probabilities on one hand and deductive entailment and inconsistency on the other, and

[7] Neither of these explanations amounts to much because neither is sufficiently broad or deep — we want to know why bodies accelerate at the rate mentioned, and why most albino cats are deaf. This cause of dissatisfaction, however, has nothing to do with our difference between certain and probable explanation.

have shown how the most salient differences between them are fairly to be described as differences of degree. If our doubter demur that our probabilities nevertheless are *not* entailments or inconsistencies, we are glad to agree. If he denies that they are 'logical' connections in the same sense as are entailment and inconsistency, he has been definitely shown wrong to the extent that they are similarly analytic and intrinsic, that they are definable in terms of the primitive ideas necessary and sufficient for developing the standard system of logic and mathematics, and that they are pertinent to the truth values of their antecedents and consequents in the same way as are entailment and inconsistency. If he merely intends to refuse to call any implicative relation except entailment and inconsistency a 'logical' relation, the burden is on him to prove that he is adopting an idiosyncrasy of vocabulary any more helpful than would be a resolve to use "temperature" only for a *hot* say of 12,000,000° C. and a *cold* of absolute zero, and not for any degree in between.

Anyone who would bring us to doubt the propriety of our intermediate implications must do so, then, on the ground that the logical respects in which they are analogous to entailment but of less degree are somehow not the respects essential for the actual justification of belief — that they lack the claim upon us which entailment has. If the person who expresses this doubt means merely an introspective report that our probabilities do not touch his nerve, do not move him to acquiescence, his statement is irrelevant if true, but it is probably not true. It is irrelevant because no logical principle is psychologically compulsive; every principle leaves a man free to ignore it at his own risk. It is probably not true because there are few or no dissenters more ready in practice, whatever their theoretical qualms, to refrain from belief and action in accordance with probabilities than in accordance with the rest of logic. The worst which our gadfly can do, therefore, is to allege that we cannot give the same kind of practical reason for believing propositions which are merely probable in relation to given evidence as we can for believing such as are entailed by it.

Granted that it is desirable that our beliefs should be true, both because truth is good in itself and because true beliefs are the means for attaining other goods, probabilities not only do not guarantee the same amount of profit as entailments; they do not guarantee any at all. This demurrer, strained and rare, turns out to be as fundamental and fascinating as anything in the lists of philosophy and to touch at one point or another most of the principal confusions and refusals which have bedeviled the whole theory of probability.

There can be no doubt of the profit, theoretical or practical, at once and in the long run, of believing demonstrative propositions and rejecting impossible ones. Any one proposition which is demonstrated with certainty must be true and any one disproved with certainty must be false, while all of any collection of demonstrated propositions must likewise be true and none of any collection of impossible propositions can be true. Now, no one would expect that belief in merely probable propositions (propositions established with probabilities, say, greater than .5 but less than 1.0) should infallibly guarantee the same amount of profit, in the single instance or in the long run, as does a belief in demonstrated propositions. Since probability is not a degree of truth, no one of good sense would demand, either, that belief in a proposition whose probability, say, is .8 should infallibly confer just .8 of the satisfaction which would be conferred if the proposition were demonstrated. There seems a certain justice, however, in the stipulation that if probabilities are to create an obligation or inducement of the same kind as that created by an entailment, then a steadfast adherence to probable propositions should infallibly in the long run result in an amount of profit proportionate to the probability. That is, although we cannot be sure that in believing any one merely probable proposition we must be right or even partly right, we ought to be sure that by persistently believing in highly probable propositions we shall be right more frequently than if we believed improbable ones.

At first there appears no difficulty about that. We know by

observation that beliefs based on high probabilities are in fact
more often true and actions based on highly probable beliefs
are more often successful than those based on low probabilities
or sheer guesses. So far, however, this is not a logical guarantee
but an empirical generalization; it cannot justify a logical procedure but must be justified by a logical procedure. A better,
and strictly logical, guarantee seems to be furnished by our
description of highly probable conclusions as of necessity and
by definition members of classes of propositions of which the
most are true. This, however, does not mean that most of the
conclusions which I actually draw must be true unless I draw all
the conclusions in those classes. Given a bag of 1000 marbles
of which 900 are red, for example, there is a probability of .9
that any one named or selected marble is red. If now I work
down through the bagful, naming or selecting all the marbles
one by one and asserting of each marble that it is red, my assertion is bound to be true in just $\frac{9}{10}$ of the cases, but that is a
negligibly rare and useless procedure. Our probability inferences
seldom or never exhaust any one of the reference classes by
which 'the' probabilities are determined, but select rather one
or two cases from each of many reference classes. Our daily
situation, in other words, is as if we selected, not all the marbles
from a bagful of 1000 in which .9 are red, but one marble apiece
from 1000 bagfuls in each of which about .9 are red. Each marble
then is known to be a member of a class in which .9 are red, but
there does not follow demonstratively that in the cross-class of
1000 marbles which are actually selected .9 must be red. These
might all be red, or none red; our conclusions, each with a probability of .9, might with good luck all be true, and with very bad
luck they might all be false.

The most we can say in the circumstances mentioned is that
it is *highly probable* that the actual proportion of successes will
be approximately the same as the single probabilities, namely .9.
This follows by the multiplicative and additive laws of probability and is equivalent to the logical law of large numbers
which we are to investigate in the next chapter. In effect it

means that a person's probability inferences throughout his lifetime will very probably succeed with a relative frequency approximately equal to their average probability: the higher the separate probabilities, the more often he will probably succeed, while the more numerous his inferences, the greater the probability that he will succeed with that frequency. Normally, indeed, the probability that he will be right with a relative frequency approximately equal to the average probability is much greater than the average probability itself. Nevertheless, that assurance never mounts to a demonstrative guarantee. A massing of probabilities may in the manner shown generate a greater probability, but it can never deliver a certainty, and every probability thus generated is subject in turn to the same criticism — there is no certainty, but only a probability again, that it will be cashed in an actual frequency of successes, that, to use the old gambling phrase, it will 'mature'. Knowing that 90 per cent of the marbles in a bag are red, I am on our theory reasonably inclined to guess *red* rather than *not-red* with respect to any one marble. If I doubt the reasonableness of this inclination I can argue that there is a probability of .99, let us say, that by this method I shall guess right at least 90 per cent of the time in a long series of such conclusions. This assurance, however, is itself of the same kind with the first one — it means that I can expect such a ratio of successes with the same logical warrant as that with which I could expect a single marble to be red if it were selected from a bag containing red marbles in the ratio .99; and so forth. If the first marble ratio does not *ipso facto* constitute a full-blooded reason for guessing red rather than not-red, neither do any of the subsequent probabilities.

Here we are up against the very nub and quick of graded credibility and, indeed, of knowledge, a topic in comparison with which most principles of divinity or mathematics are derivative and frivolous. All too little has been said about it by others and we can here say little more. The fact that adherence to high probabilities promises only a probability of even a balance of profit has moved some recent writers (Jeffreys and

Reichenbach for example) to append to their axioms of probability the special postulate or rule of 'positing', presumably analogous to the rule of inference appended by the mathematical logicians to their transformation formulas, that nevertheless we 'ought to' or 'shall' believe more probable propositions in preference to less probable ones. Such a rule cannot be wrong, but I am inclined to think its special statement is unnecessary and misleading. For it stands to reason — in the sense that syllogistic probabilities are intuitively satisfactory without demonstrative guarantee of maturation, that the demand for a demonstrative guarantee is logically absurd, and that no theory of probability can or does promise it.

Intuitively we accept statistical probabilities every day and every hour, without thinking about their maturation and unruffled by the reflection that their maturation is not certain. We know that there is some net final risk in even the best and most diversified portfolio of investments, pecuniary or philosophical. We know perfectly well that there is such a thing as bad luck, an occasional persistent failure to hit the mark in spite of all humanly possible precautions. This is too bad, but anything else is repugnant to good sense: it remains none the less reasonable to wager our lives and fortunes where our chances are best. The lifelong situation of each of us is like that of a man confronted on the Judgment Day with two urns filled with black and white lots, told that there are a million white to one black in the first urn and a million black to one white in the second, and required to choose an urn, and a lot from it, on the condition that if he chooses a black lot he shall go to hell forever and if he chooses a white one he shall go to heaven. In our mundane lives the choice lies between a consistent adherence to the rule of greatest probability and a rejection of it. In both cases it is overwhelmingly more probable that the one recourse will bring advantage than that the other will, although in both cases by hypothesis the possibility of subsequent maturation is ruled out. To put the question of what the reasonable man will do in either set of circumstances is to answer it: if he did not choose the first urn, we should consider him mad or illogical in the same way and almost in the same degree as though he offended strict syllogistic propriety by preferring an urn in which *all* the lots were black to one in which *none* was.

Logically, we have observed, the demand that a congeries of probabilities should generate a certainty is self-contradictory, and contradictory of the very concept of graded credibility. From the principle definitive of "probability" itself, that given 'the' probability of any one proposition, no matter how high, it may be false, there follows by simple logical rules that given a similar probability for each of any number of propositions, however high, they *may* be all false, or all true, or false and true in any proportion whatever. This has long been the burden of the standard critique of 'the gambler's fallacy' and the Bernoullian 'bridge'. The gambler's fallacy is the belief, reputedly held and practiced by gamblers, that 'the chances must mature' — that if there is a probability of $\frac{m}{n}$ for a specified result at roulette, say, then the player who keeps on a long while must get that result $\frac{m}{n}$ of the time, and if the wheel falls short of that figure for a while it is bound by 'the laws of probability' or 'the law of averages' to reverse the trend and even things up. One and perhaps the only logical justification for this has been supposed to be Bernoulli's theorem, or some similar mathematical law of large numbers, understood as supplying a bridge from the prior probability of a specified kind of event to the subsequent frequency of its occurrence. The vanity of this hope, as we pointed it out above, has often been pointed out by others: the theorem can derive from the initial probability a probability for subsequent frequencies but never a certainty.

The absurdity of hoping for a certainty in such circumstances has been concealed perhaps by the imaginability of situations where in some peculiar manner we do happen to know what will be the frequency of our successes and that the frequency will correspond to the probability. This was the case where we supposed ourselves knowing the ratio of red marbles in the bag and then asserting of every marble *seriatim* that it is red. This

possibility does not contradict our principle that probabilities
do not generate certainties, because our certainty of a specified
success frequency is here not deduced from the single probability of success but from further knowledge of the peculiar
conditions of the drawing. An assurance at first sight less
trivial seems promised by the converse expedient of defining
'the probability' of a certain kind of conclusion, in relation to a
certain kind of premise, as consisting in or determined by the
relative frequency of success in my actual inferences of that
variety. If I knew, for example, that in all my marble guessing,
from birth to death, I was fated to succeed two times out of
three, I could impute to my next guess now a probability of $\frac{2}{3}$
which I knew would mature. I could have no such knowledge,
however, except by some strange sort of clairvoyance, and since
it would be possible even then only if all my choices were already
decided it would be worthless to tell me how to choose. One
proof that a guarantee of maturity is not essential to a valid
probability is that if I did know concerning a marble which I
have just guessed to be red, not only that two-thirds of all my
marble guesses forever are doomed to be true but that this
marble is just taken from a bag in which 99 per cent are red, I
should adjust my confidence and demand betting odds to match
the latter information rather than the former, although the
former guarantees a maturity and the latter does not.

Philosophically, since the refusal to guarantee the maturity
of the chances is a consequent of the bare concept of graded
credibility itself, our account of probability naturally enough
is not in this respect at a disadvantage as against the other
theories of probability. If it seems so, this can only be because
it is simpler and less equivocal and hence enables us to be clearly
aware of the matter as the others do not. The subjectivistic
theory and the intuitionist theory, so far as they depart from
our classic doctrine by announcing probabilities which are not
based on statistical ratios at all, have on their hands not merely
the problem of passing from a known statistical ratio to a success frequency in a subsequent series of trials or inferences but

the much darker problem of passing from an essentially non-statistical probability connection to any frequency whatever. The frequency theory of probability does not present this double problem, and has been often cited as superior to the classic theory on the ground that it meets the demand for maturation as the other does not. What it promises, we remember, is that the probability of a given inference will mature in the infinitely long run because the probability *is* the relative frequency of successes of that kind of inference in the infinitely long run. This is a vain boast because in the first place there is no such infinitely long run of inferences. In the second place, if we accept in lieu of the infinite series the indefinitely long run of inferences which actually will take place in the course of world history, its statistical composition is even more thoroughly unknowable than that of the merely lifelong series which we rejected in the preceding paragraph, and much less knowable than any one instance, *a*, whose probability we are asking. Finally, even if such a series existed and were known it would be useless for the present purpose because a knowledge of the relative frequency of successes in an infinitely long run no more enables me to predict categorically the frequency of successes in the relatively short run of my inferences than does a knowledge of our classic kind of probability. If I knew somehow that in the infinitely long run red marbles are drawn from a certain sort of bag with a relative frequency converging on a limit of $\frac{2}{3}$, it would be highly probable that the marbles which I draw in my little part of that endless carnival will be red in a ratio near to $\frac{2}{3}$, but it would still be wholly possible that all my marbles, or none of them, will be red. Charles Peirce tried to save what he considered requisite to the rationality of probable belief by the drastic method of postulating, first, that the human race will last forever, in order that there shall be infinitely long runs, and second, that the human race is One, so that the eventual successes of mankind on the whole can give significance to my probabilities now.[8] Even Peirce, however, could not pretend by

[8] *Collected Papers*, Vol. II, pp. 395 ff., and Vol. V, p. 221.

this ruse to explain how we could meantime know any such probability, and most persons will regard his bit of metaphysics as proving that the demand that probabilities be necessarily realized in experience is a fantasy.

A person who objected to our verdict on the Doomsday choice of urns imagined on a previous page might plead that there is no ground for choice unless, at least, we know that the contents are mixed or 'randomized'. Otherwise, for all we know, the few black lots might be on top in the first urn and the few white ones on top in the second. The answer of course is that to be sure they *might*, just as they might be arranged in any of innumerable other ways, but that the existence of these bare possibilities is included in what we mean when we grant that it is only very probable that we shall be saved if we choose from the first urn and lost if we choose from the second, and not absolutely certain. The suggestion, however, introduces us to the second source of doubt of the adequacy of the statistical syllogism in general, the notion that its probabilities are subject to special assumptions concerning randomness, lack of bias, equal probability, and the like. Since those assumptions could never be tested without our making in the testing further assumptions of the same sort, the admission that they are required would be fatal to all probabilities together. The demand for randomness is closely related at several points to the demand for maturity and is to be shown invalid in somewhat the same way, by observing how it is in conflict with the very idea of graded credibility, on our theory or on any theory.

In a concrete example the objection would run thus: given that one-third of Americans are home owners and that John Jones is an American, we cannot attribute a probability of $\frac{1}{3}$ to the proposition that John Jones is a home owner *unless* we are assured that the situation is 'fair' or 'random' or 'without bias'. Now, on one interpretation, suggested by Peirce's stipulation that there must be 'no countervailing considerations',[9] this requirement is harmless but redundant: that we cannot validly

[9] *Collected Papers*, Vol. II, p. 435.

count as 'the' probability of the cited conclusion the probability determined by the one statistical syllogism in question if we have other relevant information. Relevant information in the present instance and in our terms would consist in knowledge (*a*) that John Jones is a member of some specifiable other class than just the class of Americans and (*b*) that the incidence of home ownership in that class has a specifiable value different from $\frac{1}{3}$. (The information would not be relevant, be it observed, unless it contained both of these components.) The stipulation is harmless thus understood because it is simply a restatement of the essential peculiarity of graded credibility, its relativity, that 'the' probability of a proposition may be different as different evidence prevails. For the same reason it is redundant, because every formula of probability logic, as we know, decrees just the probability relation which holds to a stated kind of consequent from a stated kind of antecedent *alone*, and not what holds from some other and more inclusive kind of antecedent. In this, the proper sense of the word, a probability inference is 'unbiased' unless its bias is known, and if its bias is known we possess the basis for a new and unbiased probability inference.

Very different from the harmless demand that the inference not be known 'biased' in the sense that it not ignore relevant evidence is the demand that it be known to be 'unbiased' in some ulterior more positive and complex sense tantamount to requiring that we know that there exist no further facts which, if they were in evidence, would be relevant. This kind of demand, for all its popularity, is seldom or never precisely expressed. In one version, however, it appears to mean that we must know, before we draw our inference, not only the ratio of Ps among the Ms but also that the Ps are 'spread around at random' among the Ms. In common speech this has some meaning, suggestive of shuffling cards or scattering seeds on a lawn. Logically it is very difficult to construe, but to promise any appreciable benefit it must intend something like this: before we accept our statistical probability we must know that the reference class M is 'homogeneous' or 'unstratified' with respect to P in the sense that in every part or subclass of it P occurs with the same relative frequency as in M as a whole, or at any rate that it does so in every part or subclass of which the moot individual a is a member. In statistical parlance, we demand to know that there is no character with which home ownership, for example, is 'associated' positively or negatively within the class of Americans, or at any rate that our individual John Jones has no such character.[10] We could thus validly attribute 'the' probability of $\frac{1}{3}$ to the proposition that John Jones is a home owner only if we knew that not only in the class of Americans but in the class of Methodists, the class of blue-eyed creatures, the class of blue-eyed ambidextrous Methodists, the class of rich Elks, and so on *ad infinitum*, the relative frequency of home ownership was uniformly $\frac{1}{3}$.

These demands, instead of being harmless and redundant like the first, are extortionate and self-contradictory. Not only is it impossible for us to know the relative frequency of P in all the subclasses of M, or even in all the subclasses of which a is a member; we know *a priori* that unless all or no M is P it is impossible that those frequencies should all be the same, with each other and with the frequency in M. When we say that one-third of Americans are home owners we are saying that there is one part of the class of Americans, namely the third, of which all are home owners, another part (the two-thirds) of which none is a home owner, and innumerable other parts, variously overlapping these, which exemplify innumerable other proportions in the range between 0 and 1. The members of each of these subclasses must share some common and peculiar property which is accordingly associated with home ownership within the generic class of Americans. If then *per impossibile* we knew the relative frequency of P within every subclass of M

---

[10] To go the whole way with the randomists we might have to require that the relative frequency of home ownership is $\frac{1}{3}$ in *all* the classes of which Jones is a member and not merely in the subclasses of Americans of which he is a member. If the latter however can be shown absurd, the former is absurd *a fortiori*.

of which *a* is a member, we should know with certainty whether *a* is *P*, since as soon as we knew of even one such subclass in which *all* or *none* is *P*, and there must be some such, all the other frequencies would be irrelevant and we should know once and for all that *a* is (or is not) *P*. Far from being requisite to the validity of probability inference, therefore, this sort of denunciation of bias is a repudiation of probability altogether and leaves us again crying for the moon of certainty.

A more moderate interpretation of the rule of randomness is that we must be assured, not that the proportion of *P* shall be the same in all the subclasses of *M* as it is in *M*, but that it shall be the same in the class of actual selections or inferences which we are going to make. With or without the additional stipulation that the *P*s be distributed among the selections in a higgledy-piggledy way, this is perhaps the most nearly official interpretation of the common prescription that our individual *a* be selected 'by a random method'. We then are allowed to count the relative frequency of home owners among Americans, say $\frac{1}{3}$, as providing the probability that John Jones, an American, is a home owner, only if in a lifetime of selecting Americans for judgment in this respect we are sure of hitting on home owners in the same proportion, $\frac{1}{3}$.

Now, this idea that a probability reckoned from an imaginary selection-series is logically worth more than one reckoned from an actual flesh-and-blood population, like that of American citizens — that the real population, indeed, if it is significant at all, is significant only as a kind of shadowy precursor of the selection-series — has been a veritable obsession among recent writers on our subject. I think that it is a fallacy, and the father and grandfather of fallacies, but certainly it calls for the most exacting scrutiny on the part of anyone who wishes to make a go of the philosophy and logic of induction. When it is carried to the length of substituting the selection-series for the prior population altogether, it becomes identical with the ill-starred frequency theory which we have discussed elsewhere. If it only demands that the prior population-frequency be known to be duplicated in the selection-series, it is apparently more moderate but it is no less questionable. Even if the prescription could be filled, what could it contribute to our credibility? Knowing the population, we already knew one class of which our man Jones is a member and in which the proportion of home owners is $\frac{1}{3}$. If we knew that in the series of our choices there is to be a *different* proportion of home owners, the information would be relevant in the sense that it would supersede with a new probability 'the' probability provided by the first information; but since by our present hypothesis the new proportion is to be the same as the old, it is not in the ordinary sense relevant at all. A probability derived from the new proportion, furthermore, is not of a new quality immune to the old discomfiture. Just as before, we do not specifically know any properties possessed by our selection of John Jones which are associated positively or negatively, in the selection-series, with home ownership, nor just how they are associated, but we nevertheless know perfectly well that there are countless such properties, among them some which altogether determine the object of our selection to be a home owner or not to be one, as the case may be, — exactly the kind of circumstance which, with respect to the class of Americans, was our motive for seeking the solace of randomness in the first place. If the additional requisition that the series be higgledy-piggledy means that P must not be associated with other properties in the series, it is as self-contradictory as our former demand for homogeneity in the class M. If it means something less than that, it is useless. Whatever virtue would reside in the knowledge that the frequency of P among our actual choices is the same as in M is due to its guaranteeing the maturity of these particular chances. Conversely, therefore, the demand for it involves also the paradoxes we have already seen to attach to the idea of guaranteeing such maturity. First, there seldom actually exists any considerable series of inferences about members of a pertinent reference class $M;$ I am very unlikely, for example, to use my statistics about American home ownership to reckon a probability concerning

many, or any, Americans except John Jones. Secondly, if there
did exist such a series, or if we allowed ourselves to speak cryp-
tically of what the series would be if there were one, it could not
possibly be known except by inductive extrapolation from previous ventures (which on the present philosophy would be left
without logical justification) or by complete enumeration (which
would be possible only when the choices were all over and the
figures therefore worthless). Finally, no vaguely long-run frequency can guarantee a lifetime maturity anyhow.

Equivalent to the rule of randomness with respect to the
statistical syllogism is the rule generally attached to the familiar
Laplacean definition of "probability" by possible and favorable
cases, that the cases must be 'equiprobable'. Like the rule of
randomness this is harmless and superfluous if it means that we
must not estimate 'the' probability of throwing an odd number
with a die merely on the basis of knowledge that the die will
fall with one of six numbers on top and that three of these are
odd, *if* we have other evidence relevant to that result — evidence, for example, that the die is loaded opposite the four, or
inductive evidence that in previous throws it or a similar die
has turned up even numbers more often than odd. In this sense
again the cases are known to be 'equally probable' unless they
are known not to be equally probable, and if they are known
not to be equally probable, we have a new probability for the
impending event and the rule of cases is not falsified but merely
inapplicable. Any more exigent demand for equiprobability,
on the other hand, leads into the same kinds of contradiction
and futility as the more exigent rules of randomness. It is
absurd to ask, for example, that we know that there *do not exist*
any facts pertaining to the cases (the sides of the die) which
affect the result of the throw in question, because, first, we could
not possibly know about all such facts, but secondly, we do
know that there *are* such facts — and that relatively to all the
facts it is either certain or impossible that the throw in question
will yield an odd number. It is hardly less absurd to demand
again that we know already that the cases are 'equiprobable'

in the sense that they will in fact turn up equally frequently in a long run of throws. In the first place, we cannot possibly know this except with a probability, either derived from a knowledge of the structure of the die or derived from observation of its past behavior, which must be accepted without such special grace. In the second place, again, although it might by hypothesis guarantee an eventual maturation of the one set of chances, it would leave us meantime in the same dubiety about the single throw as before.

The principle that a selection is fair unless it is known not to be fair, and that cases are equiprobable unless they are known not to be equiprobable, is sometimes called "the principle of indifference" or "the principle of non-sufficient reason". Strictly, we have seen, it is not a special principle but a truistic consequence of the nature of graded credibilities. The objections to it always consist in fancying situations in which the alternatives are not indifferent because there is extra evidence, but because there is extra evidence the principle does not apply and the objections are consequently irrelevant. The principle looks to some casual eyes like a method of 'deriving knowledge from ignorance'. In truth, however, it is just the contrary. It is the rule for calculating the bearing on our conclusion of the propositions which we know, irrespective of what might have been the bearing on that conclusion of propositions which we do not know. The critic of indifference and not its champion tries to wring the blood of knowledge from the turnip of ignorance when he would allude to possible but unknown disequilibria to modify or discredit our knowledge, and in so doing he contradicts himself and the most fundamental of all rules of probability logic, that 'the' probability of any proposition is its probability in relation to the known premises and them only. The principle of indifference becomes paradoxical and insufferable only when it is understood to mean that in the absence of evidence to the contrary we can be sure that the cases will in the long run be realized with equal frequency or, more specifically, that the chances must mature. To believe any such proposition would indeed be to expect to derive knowledge from ignorance on a prodigious scale, but we have resolutely spurned it.

Although persons who write and speak of the paradoxes supposedly incurred by the principle of indifference or by the classic theory of probability often have in mind nothing less innocuous than the fact, which we have just discussed, that the theory permits the same proposition to have different probabilities in relation to different antecedents, there is a more serious allegation, sometimes made, that in some situations the theory assigns to the same proposition different probabilities in relation to the same (or equivalent) antecedents. This objection is invited when there appear to be many equally legitimate ways of identifying and counting the fundamental cases, as when we try to enumerate the colors in a spectrum. The puzzle is especially appealing in the form of Bertrand's paradox, or where a 'rate' is involved. If we mark off the scale of specific densities (each the ratio of a mass to a volume) into 'equal' stretches, presumably all with equal probabilities, the corresponding scale of specific volumes (each the ratio of a volume to a mass) will be unequally divided, and conversely. The same problem, however, arises in principle when we calculate simple spatial areas: other things equal, is a mentioned person just as likely to be an inhabitant of Great Britain as he is to be an inhabitant of continental Europe, or as he is to be an inhabitant of France? Various devices have been proposed to avoid these difficulties, none of them entirely successful. If the paradoxes affect the classic theory more than any other, however, they affect it primarily in those versions which count qualities (including locations) and propositions, and not in our version, which need count only rounded-off and identifiable individuals, like marbles or men. When we derive the probability that a certain marble has a specific gravity s from the datum that it is one of a collection of marbles among which 38 per cent have that specific gravity, there is no impediment in the reflection that the scale of specific gravities is a continuum which different conventions of measurement would divide differently. When Peirce surmised

a state of total ignorance about the color of the hair of the natives
of Saturn, he could well be staggered to compute the probability
that it lies in any one stretch of the color pyramid, but if he
knew that 75 per cent of them had red hair, he would meet no
corresponding difficulty in concluding that there is a probability
of $\frac{3}{4}$ that some one specified Saturnian has red hair. There remains only the possibility that we may sometimes, in agronomy,
for example, want to make inductions about areas of a physical
continuum. In that case, however, we cannot even begin our
induction until we have canvassed the sample, and then we must
have stipulated some unequivocal *principium individuationis* or
mode of partitioning, and can validly extend our induction to
the population of segments determined by the same *principium*.
There is opportunity here still, perhaps, for hard and rewarding
thought, but it will be wasted so long as we pretend that the
question is a liability of only one kind of probability theory.

The problem of randomness, like the problem of maturity,
comes more sharply to mind in connection with our classic
account of probability than in connection with other theories
of the subject, but for the same reason — that our theory is
sufficiently clear-cut and practicable to make possible the raising
of questions about it. The nature and purport of randomness,
that is, must eventually be settled in connection with the non-
statistical theories as well as ours, with whatever extra difficulties
are created by the gulf which in those theories may separate any
credibility from any statistical distribution.

To recapitulate, I hope in this and the preceding chapter to
have shown sufficiently, or so far as this ultimate sort of question
allows, in what consists the credibility conferred by logical
principles in general, and how and why a statistical syllogism
comprises a credibility relation of the same quality as an entailment or inconsistency but susceptible of intermediate degrees.
We have observed that in no decisive point does any of the
other recognized theories of probability oppose a bar to our
traditional doctrine, and that the two most impressive charges
which can be raised to try our confidence, namely, that our

syllogisms require supplement by guarantees of maturity and randomness, are in one sense absurd and self-contradictory and in another trivial and harmless.

To show up now in effective relief the result of our study of how either a categorical or a statistical syllogism provides a genuine *reason* for accepting its conclusion, we may contrast our analysis with the false sophistication which sometimes asserts nowadays that the acceptance of logic and its consequents, deductive or inductive, is a variety of faith or dogma with no better standing, absolutely, than the religionist's faith or dogma that the world matches with his predilections. On the contrary, of course, it is just as the antithesis of reliance on logic and science that "faith" and "dogma" are significantly defined. The difference can be concealed by using those words arbitrarily to mean simply *what is believed*, but it cannot be canceled. The difference between beliefs adopted by a disciplined use of logical principles which, with ever more exactness, have been proved involved in the nature of truth and fact *per se*, and beliefs which rise and run their course from some other motive — hope, or terror, or the reverie of devout imagination — is the deepest and most enduring in the whole reach of human activity. Nor does the introduction of probability alongside demonstration affect the prerogatives of logic. Though the mystagogue hastens to interpret as a confession of faith the scientist's admission that his results are only probable, the principles of probability we have seen to be as objective, necessary, and peremptory as the rest of logic. To accept a conclusion as highly probable is in its lowest terms to accept it because it is known to be one of a class of propositions nearly all of which are true. Sheer faith, by contrast, consists in blindly plumping for one proposition out of a myriad alternatives among which all but one must be false. To equate faith with probable belief is no less absurd in principle than equating it with allegiance to wholly demonstrative truth.

With the analysis of graded credibility thus provided we are ready to ask after the credibility of induction. Since we can hardly hope to have settled the business of probability theory altogether, however, it may be useful to point out that the fortunes of our further argument do not wholly depend on acceptance of our description of the kinship of probability and the other logical relations. In the first place, even if we were forced to recant the doctrine that a proportional syllogism has 'the same kind' of logical force as the Aristotelian syllogism or a mathematical demonstration, it might still have ample force, and logical force, and I would still contend that to aver that the premise that a bag of marbles contains 9,999 white and 1 black gives no rational support to the belief that a marble abstracted from it will be white, is strictly absurd. But in the second place, if we renounced, at least for the time being, all conviction that the statistical syllogism yields a genuine credibility, or even doubted that logic itself is valid, it would remain true that nearly all persons who have tried to prove that induction has a probability have in fact understood probability to be determined by a principle equivalent to the statistical syllogism. What is very commonly called "the problem of induction", then, is to show how an induction has that kind of character in a high degree. If we can solve it we shall at worst be solving one notable problem, and portraying the profile of induction from a particularly telling angle.

4

THE PROBABILITY OF INDUCTION

In what we may call 'the inductive situation' we are interested in a class, genus, or population, M, say the class of rabbits, and we wish to know the composition of that class with respect to some property, P, say whiteness. That is, we wish to know the proportion of rabbits which are white, or the ratio of the number of white rabbits to the total number of rabbits. Using the convention that "$[M]$" stands for *the number of the class M*, we may put it that we wish to ascertain the ratio $\dfrac{[MP]}{[M]}$. What we have to go on is a knowledge of the composition, in the specified respect, of a subclass, species, or sample of that class, MQ. That is, what we know is the ratio $\dfrac{[MQP]}{[MQ]}$. So far as logic is concerned the subclass MQ may be any class included in the class M. The kind of subclass, however, on which our empirical knowledge in fact eventually rests is the *observed* part of the class M — the subclass of those rabbits, for example, which have sufficiently come under our eye so that by a summary or perfect induction we have ascertained directly the proportion which are white. (Since virtually all material knowledge rests on induction, and all induction rests on summary or perfect induction, it is a graceless error to describe perfect induction as in some invidious sense 'trivial'.) The problem of induction is the problem of finding the exact nature and the logical warrant of

the inference which concludes to the composition of the population (rabbits) from the premises or evidence afforded by the
sample (examined rabbits).

The rule of induction normally followed is to ascribe the *same*
composition to the population as is discovered in the sample.
That is, we proceed as if on the principle that, probably and
approximately,

$$\frac{[MP]}{[M]} = \frac{[MQP]}{[MQ]}.$$

Given that 20 per cent of the observed rabbits are white, we
infer that in all likelihood about 20 per cent of all rabbits are
white. When occasionally we infer that the population differs
from the sample in a specifiable way, as when we infer that
the apples in the bottom of the barrel will be inferior to
those on top, this is because of previous wider inductions,
inductions about merchandising methods, for instance, which
do proceed on the principle that populations are like their
samples. Apparently then any specific induction involves
(1) a general over-all premise, common to all inductions,
that samples 'match' their populations, and (2) specific premises peculiar to the induction immediately concerned, that
the presented class (say of observed rabbits) is a sample of a
population (say of rabbits) and that its composition with
respect to a specified property (say whiteness) is so-and-so
(say 20 per cent). Given these premises, it follows demonstratively that, probably and approximately, the proportion of
rabbits which are white is 20 per cent. Of the premises thus
utilized, the last one, concerning the composition of the sample,
is established by observation. The next to the last, that the
class of observed rabbits is a subclass of the class of rabbits, is
an analytic truism, an instance of the logical law of subsumption,
that any class product *PQ* necessarily is contained in either of
the component classes, say *P*. All that remains then to justify
an induction of this form is to establish the first and most
abstract premise, that any population will probably and approxi-

mately match, in any statistical respect, any of its samples —
or at any rate that it will do so under certain verifiable conditions. If this, which may be called 'the inductive principle',
can be exactly stated and can be proved analytically and demonstratively, like the principle of the syllogism, and not merely
inductively, it will provide at least one sufficient solution of the
problem of induction. The sole *material* premise then required
for a valid induction is a statement of the size and composition
of the sample.

In effect, the solution of the problem of induction which I
here defend is a statement and proof of the above inductive
principle. We shall understand its significance better, however, and make surer that it grows out of a fair canvass of the
problem, if we return to the concrete demands of the inductive
situation and work it out from there.

No demonstrative principle, either the Aristotelian syllogism
or the latest dodge of the mathematical logician, will avail us,
we know, to infer directly from the composition of MQ to the
composition of M. Given that 99 out of 100 MQs are P, we
cannot with certainty deduce anything about what proportion
of Ms are P except that the sheer number of Ms which are P
must be at least as great as the number of MQs which are P.
It remains logically possible that none of the rest of the Ms is
P and that all of them are and that any intermediate proportion
are. We must be content then with a probability, preferably a
high probability, if we are to ground any inference from the
composition of a sample to the composition of its population.

It is equally apparent, however, that the ordinary proportional syllogism will not furnish directly the required probability.
Given our premise that 99 per cent of MQ is P, we can state
syllogistically the probability that any particular member of
MQ, say a, is P, and by means of the additive and multiplicative
laws we can reckon the probability that any selected group of
members of MQ, say the sub-subclass MQR, will all be P, or
that half will be P, and so forth, but all these inferences are
purely explicative. They tell us about individuals and classes

included in the sample *MQ;* they tell us nothing about the object
of our ampliative induction, the population *M*, which includes
but is not included in *MQ*.

There is a clue for us here nevertheless. If we imagine the
inductive situation reversed, so that instead of knowing already
the composition of the sample *MQ* and trying to infer the composition of the population *M*, we know the composition of the
population *M* and try to infer what will be the composition of a
sample *MQ* drawn from it, the proportional syllogism with its
auxiliaries will do the job. For simplicity's sake let the population *M* be a bagful of marbles. (We shall see later that induction
is, if anything, more difficult to justify in these artificial situations than on the wider stage of concrete scientific inquiry, so
that whatever we can establish with respect to the simple bag
of marbles will be valid *a fortiori* for more cumbrous populations
of atoms, planets, labor unionists, and so forth.) Let *MP* be the
red marbles, and let the sample *MQ* be a handful of marbles
scooped from the bag. Now, if we knew that all the marbles in
the bag were red, i.e., that

$$\frac{[MP]}{[M]} = 1,$$

or that none was red, i.e., that

$$\frac{[MP]}{[M]} = 0,$$

we could infer by the traditional *dictum de omni et nullo*, in a
demonstrative syllogism, that the same must be true of the
handful *MQ*. That is, if all the marbles in the bag are red, and
the handful consists of marbles in the bag, then all the handful
must be red, and if none of the marbles in the bag is red, certainly none of the handful can be red. These are old-fashioned
syllogisms in the moods Barbara and Celarent with universal
minor premises instead of the singular ones with which we were
made familiar by Chapter 2. If now some intermediate proportion of the marbles in the bag are known to be red, if $\frac{2}{3}$ are red,
let us say, we must resort to a proportional instead of a cate-

gorical syllogism, and be content with a probability. By itself, to be sure, the proportional syllogism, with its singular minor premise and singular conclusion, enables us under the circumstances only to state the probability that any one marble in our handful will be red. Since every member of the handful (*MQ*) is a member of the bagful (*M*), and since the proportion of red marbles in the bagful is $\frac{2}{3}$, the probability that any specified member of the handful will be red is $\frac{2}{3}$. By means of the multiplicative and additive laws, however, which are rules for deriving the probabilities of compound propositions from the probabilities of simpler ones, we can under certain conditions use this knowledge to calculate exactly the probability that the handful will contain any stipulated proportion of red marbles, either $\frac{2}{3}$ (the same as the proportion in the bagful) or any other proportion we care to name. One condition required for the reckoning is that we know the number of the handful, [*MQ*], which is generally easy; another is that we either know the total number of marbles [*M*] and the number of red marbles [*MP*], or know that these numbers are so great that the withdrawal of the handful *MQ*, whatever *its* composition may be, cannot appreciably affect the composition of what remains — or that we replace each marble before drawing the next so that our total selection cannot make any difference to the population composition. Let us suppose for a moment that one or the other of the last two conditions, which are arithmetically equivalent, is realized. The former is not a very plausible supposition with regard to a bagful of marbles, but it is a safe one with respect to the great natural populations, of rabbits, stars, or what not, with which induction is usually concerned. If for convenience' sake we consider a 'handful' of only 3 members, the probability that *all* will be red is, by the multiplicative law, $\frac{2}{3} \times \frac{2}{3} \times \frac{2}{3}$, or $(\frac{2}{3})^3$, or $\frac{8}{27}$. In general, the probability that all of a sample *MQ* will have the character *P* is equal to $\left(\dfrac{[MP]}{[M]}\right)^{[MQ]}$:

that is, it is equal to the probability of any one *M*'s being *P*, multiplied by itself to a number of terms equal to the number of

*MQ*s. Now, if the proportion of red marbles in the bag is $\frac{2}{3}$, the proportion of non-red marbles must be $1 - \frac{2}{3}$, or $\frac{1}{3}$, and the probability that any specified marble will be non-red is $\frac{1}{3}$. The probability that none of the marbles in the handful of 3 will be red is accordingly $(\frac{1}{3})^3$, or $\frac{1}{27}$. Figuring the probability that just two of the three will be red and the other non-red, so that the proportion of red in the handful will be the same as in the bagful, is a little more complicated. The probability that any designated two marbles in the handful will be red and the third not red is equal to $\frac{2}{3} \times \frac{2}{3} \times \frac{1}{3}$, or $\frac{4}{27}$. But this, of course, is not the only allotment of red and non-red among the three marbles which will give a total of two red and one not red. There are in fact three such allotments: any one of the three marbles may be the non-red one while the other two are red. Each of these allotments has the same probability, $\frac{4}{27}$, so that by the additive law the probability of obtaining some one or other of them is equal to $\frac{4}{27} + \frac{4}{27} + \frac{4}{27}$, or $\frac{4}{27} \times 3$, or $\frac{4}{9}$. This is less than an even chance, but we can note already that it is greater than the probability of any one other composition. The probability of getting one red marble and two non-red ones, for example, is only $(\frac{2}{3} \times \frac{1}{3} \times \frac{1}{3}) \times 3$, or $\frac{2}{9}$.

If now we give up our handy fiction that the population *M* (marbles in the bag) is virtually infinite, and suppose that it contains, say, 60 members, of which 40 are red, we find not a less but a greater probability that the proportion in our tiny sample will match it. The probability that the first marble in the sample will be red is $\frac{40}{60}$, but the probability then that the next marble is red is $\frac{39}{59}$, while the probability that the third marble is non-red is then $\frac{20}{58}$. The probability that *some* two marbles will be red, then, and some one non-red, is equal to $(\frac{2}{3} \times \frac{39}{59} \times \frac{10}{29}) \times 3$, or $\frac{2340}{5133}$. Decimally, this is .456, whereas $\frac{4}{9}$, our previous fraction, is only .444. In general, as the reader may be sufficiently persuaded by these examples, the effect of assuming a virtually infinite population where in fact the population is finite, is to determine a smaller probability for a matching sample than a more accurate procedure would yield. Since a calculation using the precise number of M is more complicated, and since we very seldom know the number $[M]$ anyhow, and since furthermore the difference between the results is insignificant as soon as $[M]$ is five or six times as great as $[MQ]$, as always happens in the sort of situations with which we shall be concerned, we may safely employ the simpler method. In any case the true probability cannot be less than we state.

A sample set MQ of only three members is grotesquely small. Scrutinizing our illustration, however, we hit on some general rules. Given a set or sample MQ, taken from a population M, the probability that any specified subset or part of MQ, of number n, will be P, is equal to the nth power of the proportion of Ps among the Ms, i.e., to $\left(\dfrac{[MP]}{[M]}\right)^n$. The probability that the remaining $[MQ] - n$ members of MQ will be *non-P* is $\left(1 - \dfrac{[MP]}{[M]}\right)^{[MQ]-n}$, or, if we write "$\bar{P}$" for the class or property *non-P*, it is $\left(\dfrac{[M\bar{P}]}{[M]}\right)^{[MQ]-n}$. The probability of the conjunction, that one specified subset in MQ, with n members, will be P and the rest will be *non-P*, is equal to the product of these two quantities, that is, to

$$\left(\frac{[MP]}{[M]}\right)^n \times \left(\frac{[M\bar{P}]}{[M]}\right)^{[MQ]-n}$$

We are now interested, however, not in the probability that one particular subset of n MQs will be P and the rest not P, but in the probability that just some, that is, one or another, subset of n MQs will be P and the rest not P. The number of subsets of n members each which exist in a class MQ is the number of mathematical 'combinations' of $[MQ]$ things taken n at a time, $^{[MQ]}C_n$. The probability, then, that just n members of the sample MQ will be P and that the other $[MQ] - n$ members will be not P is equal to:

$$\left(\frac{[MP]}{[M]}\right)^n \times \left(\frac{[M\bar{P}]}{[M]}\right)^{[MQ]-n} \times {}^{[MQ]}C_n.$$

Rules for reckoning the number of combinations of r things taken n at a time are included in the algebra books. One is provided by the equation

$$^rC_n = \frac{r \times (r-1) \times (r-2) \times \cdots \times ((r-n)+1)}{n \times (n-1) \times (n-2) \times \cdots \times 1}.$$

That is, for the numerator we multiply r by the next smaller number than r and so on down till we have multiplied together n numbers in all. For the denominator, we multiply n by the next less number than it and so on down to 1. Since to pick n things out of a collection of r things is at the same time to single out another set of things, whose number is $r - n$, to be left behind, the rule holds that $^rC_n = {}^rC_{r-n}$. When n is greater than $r - n$, therefore, we can save trouble by figuring on the latter rather than the former. In our first simplified example, above, we employed the fact that $^3C_2 = {}^3C_1 = 3$; the numbers of combinations involved in more ordinary instances will be enormously greater.

The notion of 'combinations' is fundamental to our whole program and must be grasped with intuitive sureness if we are to get anywhere. A combination is often referred to as a 'selection' or 'possible selection' of things. Perhaps the most familiar example of it is the notion of a hand of cards. Any given bridge hand of 13 cards is a selection from a class of 52 cards, and is one of the some billions of possible selections or combinations of 52 cards taken 13 at a time.

Now if we know again that $\frac{2}{3}$ M is P but if we take 9 individuals to compose the selected group MQ instead of only 3, the probability that just $\frac{2}{3}$ of *them*, or 6, will be P, is equal to $(\frac{2}{3})^6 \times (\frac{1}{3})^3 \times {}^9C_3$. ($^9C_3$, we remember, is the same as $^9C_6$.) This works out as $\frac{64}{729} \times \frac{1}{27} \times \frac{9 \times 8 \times 7}{3 \times 2 \times 1}$, or $\frac{64}{19683} \times 84$, or .273. The result is a little disconcerting because it is less than the probability of getting a match with the smaller sample of 3, which in decimals was .444. In point of fact, the larger the sample the less likely it is to match the population *exactly*.

When a sample is more than the merest handful, however —
and this covers all cases of inductive importance — we are not
interested in the probability of an exact match, which may indeed be impossible since the sample may not be exactly divisible
in the ratio $\frac{[MP]}{[M]}$. We want to know the probability that the
sample composition will not vary from the population composition by more than a certain percentage or proportion, and this
always does increase as the sample increases. Our sample of 9
is still far too small to be typical but even with it we can reckon
the probability of not missing the 'true' proportion by more than
11.1 per cent, i.e., one individual, one way or the other. The
probability that 7 instead of 6 of the 9 members of MQ will be P
is $(\frac{2}{3})^7 \times (\frac{1}{3})^2 \times {}^9C_2$, or $\frac{128}{19683} \times 36$, or .234. The probability
that only 5 will be P is $(\frac{2}{3})^5 \times (\frac{1}{3})^4 \times {}^9C_4$, which figures out to
.205. The probability of each of the two nearly-matching com-
positions for MQ is less than the probability of the exactly
matching composition, 6-and-3. The probability however of
getting *some one* of these three compositions which either
match or nearly match is (by the additive law) equal to .273 +
.234 + .205, or .712. Even with a tiny sample of 9, therefore,
drawn from a virtually infinite population, M, of which $\frac{2}{3}$ are P,
the probability that the proportion of Ps in the sample will not
vary from what it is in the population, namely $\frac{2}{3}$, by more than
11.1 per cent, is .712. As we consider larger samples, a near
match (in terms of percentage) becomes rapidly more probable,
or — what comes to the same thing — the probable disparity
between sample and population becomes rapidly less. By
'Bernoulli's theorem' it is accordingly always possible to specify
a sample sufficiently large so that there is as great a probability
as we please that the sample matches the population as closely
as we please. This is true for a population divided in the ratio $\frac{2}{3}$;
it is true for populations divided in other ratios, though the
probabilities of a given degree of approximation for samples
from differently divided populations are different. By a common mathematical procedure the statisticians have calculated

from principles such as we have been observing an over-all rule, for virtually infinite [M] and large [MQ], the formula for 'the standard error of sampling', $\sigma_\%$:

$$\vdash: \sigma_{\left(\frac{[MQP]}{[MQ]}\right)} = \sqrt{\frac{\frac{[MP]}{[M]} \times \frac{[M\bar{P}]}{[M]}}{[MQ]}}.$$

The standard error or 'standard deviation' got by this rule is the degree of approximation attached to the 'standard' probability, .6826. That is, there is a probability of .6826 that the composition of the sample, $\frac{[MQP]}{[MQ]}$, will not differ or 'deviate' from the composition of the population, $\frac{[MP]}{[M]}$, by an amount (i.e., by a percentage or proportion) greater than the value of σ thus computed. It is provable, furthermore, that there is a probability of .9545 that the sample will not deviate by more than $2 \times \sigma$, and a probability of .9973 that it will not diverge more than $3 \times \sigma$. Given a large population (M) of marbles, say, in which the proportion of red marbles (MP) is $\frac{2}{3}$ and the proportion of non-red marbles is accordingly $\frac{1}{3}$, and given a fairly large sample of 600 marbles, say, then $\sigma = \sqrt{\frac{\frac{2}{3} \times \frac{1}{3}}{600}}$, or $\sqrt{.000370370}$, or a little less than .02. This means that there is a probability of .6826 (the chances are about 2 to 1) that the proportion of red marbles in the sample will not differ from the proportion in the population ($\frac{2}{3}$, or 66.7 per cent) by more than 2 per cent. There is that probability, in other words, that the proportion of red marbles in the sample will lie between 64.7 per cent and 68.7 per cent. There is a probability of .9545 that the sample will not differ by more than 4 per cent, and a probability of .9973 that it will not differ by more than 6 per cent.

The deviation corresponding to a probability of .6826, called "sigma", is taken as standard only because of some important arithmetical peculiarities and because of its comparative simplicity of calculation. There are tables by which from this base there can be figured the deviation corresponding to any other probability, or the probability corresponding to any other deviation. The 'probable error' ('P.E.'), for example, is the deviation corresponding to a probability of $\frac{1}{2}$. It is equal to .6745 $\times$ σ.[1] With the deviation formulas at hand the statisticians are accustomed to calculate, for any composition of population, and for a sample of any size, the probability that the sample will match the population with any desired accuracy.

Of what use, however, we may ask, is all this? In the inductive situation we don't know the composition of the population on which all this depends — that's just what we are trying to learn. And we aren't trying to find out the composition of the sample — that's just what we know already. Practical statisticians, to be sure, commonly ignore the difference and recommend that, not knowing the composition of the population, we write for the $\frac{[MP]}{[M]}$ and $\frac{[M\bar{P}]}{[M]}$ required by the sampling formula the values observed in the sample for $\frac{[MQP]}{[MQ]}$ and $\frac{[MQ\bar{P}]}{[MQ]}$ respectively. "Standard error" is often defined to mean just this quantity. That its use is a begging of the question does not need laboring. It puts us in the position of asking absurdly, "If we assume that the population has the same composition as the sample, what is the probability that the sample will have the same composition as the population?"

---

[1] There is no special significance for our purpose in the similarity between the standard probability .6828 and the quantity .6745 which occurs in the equation relating σ to the P.E. There is no significance at all, of course, in the similarity between both of these and our illustrative population composition .667 (i.e., $\frac{2}{3}$). The σ probability is always and by definition .6826 (and a bit more), and the P.E. is always .6745 $\times$ σ (a bit less). A population composition of $\frac{2}{3}$ serves as illustration only because $\frac{2}{3}$ is a neat and easy sort of fraction. It should be clear, incidentally, that when we speak of a 'percentage deviation' we mean a percentage of the whole population or sample and not a percentage of the composition. The sigma formula itself is an idealization which actual instances only approach, but this is not a detriment because its discrepancy is only such as to overestimate the error.

The statistician's trick nevertheless gives us another important clue. In the first place, although the inferring of the
composition of the population from the composition of the
sample is not logically the same as the converse process of
inferring the composition of the sample from the composition of
the population, both inferences could be made valid by the
single general principle that given any population and any
(largish) sample thereof, it is highly probable that the sample
matches the population (and hence that the population matches
the sample). In the second place, the latter general principle
may be proved to be true by no more intricate method than
considering *the whole range of possible population compositions*
and observing that although the probability of a matching
sample of a stipulated size is different for different compositions,
the probability of a matching sample is always greater than the
probability of any other kind of sample, and if the sample is
large, then *no matter what the population composition may be,*
the probability is very great.

To bring this out clearly, let us look again at the sampling
formula and ask how much we can say about its various terms
even though we do not yet know the actual composition of the
population. We know $[MQ]$, the number of the sample.   We can
usually make it as great as we like, and the formula indicates
that the greater it is, the more nearly the sample is likely to
match the population. Of the other quantities we do not know
$\dfrac{[MP]}{[M]}$ and $\dfrac{[M\bar{P}]}{[M]}$, the composition of the population with respect
to P and to *non-P* respectively. By pure logic and arithmetic,
however, we know something about them. We know that
$\dfrac{[M\bar{P}]}{[M]}$ must be equal to
$$1 - \frac{[MP]}{[M]},$$

and we know the range within which both must lie, and hence
the range of the required product,

$$\frac{[MP]}{[M]} \times \frac{[M\bar{P}]}{[M]}.$$

In the extreme cases, the proportion of *P*s among the *M*s, $\frac{[MP]}{[M]}$, is 1 or 0; that is, all *M* is *P* or no *M* is *P;* and the proportion of *non-P*s among the *M*s will accordingly be 0 or 1, respectively. In either of these circumstances, any sample, no matter what its size, *must* match. In the sampling formula, this result appears as the fact that σ, and every multiple of σ, is then 0, while our quantity

$$\left(\frac{[MP]}{[M]}\right)^{[MQP]} \times \left(\frac{[M\bar{P}]}{[M]}\right)^{[MQ\bar{P}]} \times {}^{[MQ]}C_{[MQP]}$$

then must reduce to $1 \times 1 \times 1$. (The 0th power of any number is 1.) It is plainest, of course, by the *dictum de omni et nullo* of the categorical syllogism.

On the other hand, the probability of matching is least, and the probable deviation σ is the greatest, when the composition of the population is midway between the two extremes 0 and 1, that is, when just half of *M* is *P* and half accordingly is *non-P*,

$$\frac{[MP]}{[M]} = \frac{[M\bar{P}]}{[M]} = \frac{1}{2}.$$

In other words, the product of $\frac{1}{2} \times \frac{1}{2}$, namely, $\frac{1}{4}$, is greater than the product of any other two numbers whose arithmetical sum is 1, as the reader may satisfy himself by a few experiments, and it determines accordingly the greatest, and 'worst', value of σ. What happens then in this worst of all conceivable situations for the probability of the sample's matching the population? We might easily expect a very great deviation indeed, or a correspondingly low probability. If the best possible situation, with a parent composition of 0 or 1, makes it certain that the sample will have the matching composition, we could pessimistically conjecture, for instance, that the worst possible situation, with a parent composition of $\frac{1}{2}$, if it did not make a matching sample impossible, would make it at any rate no more probable than any other variety of sample. If such were the case, we should have got nowhere by all this inquiry. Emphatically, however, it is not the case: *the worst possible situation is still a very favorable one.* No matter what the composition of the population — even if it is half and half — the sample not only is more likely to have the matching composition than to have any other composition; it is, if it is fairly large, *very* likely to have very nearly the matching composition — a nearly matching composition, that is, is then much more probable than all the other possible compositions put together.

Filling in the σ formula with the worst possible values of $\frac{[MP]}{[M]}$ and $\frac{[M\overline{P}]}{[M]}$, and writing " $\gtreqless$ " to mean *is equal to or less than* (i.e., *is no greater than*) we have the principle,

$$\vdash : \sigma \gtreqless \sqrt{\frac{.5 \times .5}{[MQ]}}.$$

The crucial right-hand expression may of course be written also more simply as $\frac{.5}{\sqrt{[MQ]}}$. If $[MQ]$, the number of the sample, is 2500, for example, then the standard deviation *cannot* be more than $\frac{.5}{\sqrt{2500}}$, or .01. That is, there must be a probability of .6826 at the very least that the sample composition does not differ from the population composition by more than 1 per cent, and a probability, at the very least, of .9545 that it does not differ by more than twice this, or 2 per cent, and so forth. The probability that the composition of the sample does not differ from that of the population by more than 2 per cent, however, is identical with the probability that the composition of the population does not differ from that of the sample by more than 2 per cent. If now we take the actual observed composition of the sample, say $\frac{2}{3}$ *P* and $\frac{1}{3}$ *non-P*, it follows that there is a probability of *at least* .9545 that the proportion of *P*s in the population does not differ from $66\frac{2}{3}$ per cent by more than 2 per cent; i.e., there is that probability that the proportion of *P*s in the population lies between $64\frac{2}{3}$ per cent and $68\frac{2}{3}$ per cent. If this is not a high enough probability, or a small enough possible deviation, the remedy is at hand: we need only add to the sample. We cannot in this fashion reach unmitigated certainty, and since our rule connects the reliability of the inference, not directly with the number of the sample but with the square root of the number, we must continually add more generously to the sample in order to bring about a stipulated amount of increase in the reliability. We can in theory, nevertheless, approach certainty within any assignable margin, however small, and we can in practice rapidly attain a 'moral certainty' humanly indistinguishable from the result of a strict deductive demonstration (which in spite of its ideal impeccability is always subject to error due to the inadvertence of the deducer).

Here, I take it, is in main principle a solution of the problem of induction. We wished to prove that an inference from $\frac{m}{n}$ *MQ is P* to $\frac{m}{n}$ *M is P* has a genuine probability or logical credibility of the sort described in Chapter 2, and that when *MQ* is fairly numerous it has a large probability of that sort. What we have to work with in an inductive situation consists of two kinds of knowledge: the number of the sample, and its composition, which are facts of observation; and the principle that no matter what the population is like, any sample, of considerable size, will very probably be very similar to it, this being an *a priori* law of classes, demonstrable by logical analysis. Putting together these two pieces of knowledge, and taking advantage of the fact that to say that a given sample of 2502 marbles, say, of which $\frac{2}{3}$ are red, is very probably very similar in a statistical way to the total content of the much larger bagful from which it was taken, is equivalent to saying that the total bagful is very probably very similar to the sample, we conclude that in the total bagful very probably very nearly $\frac{2}{3}$ of the marbles are red. We have in fact done better: we have provided no method of laying down *exactly* how probable is any assignable degree of approximation between population and sample, but we are able to lay down a little indeterminately the minimum possible probability for any stipulated degree of approximation, or con-

versely the maximum possible divergence for any stipulated
degree of probability, by the *a priori* principle

$$\vdash: \sigma \gtreqless \frac{.5}{\sqrt{[MQ]}}.$$

To most of us, this odd margin of indeterminateness about
the inductive probability will be some earnest of the *bona fides*
of the whole calculation. Not only do we seldom or never want
to know exactly the probability of an inductive argument; we
should be suspicious, rightly or wrongly, of any scheme which
could adduce an exact probability for one. What we want, and
the most we are inclined to credit, is a whacking big probability, objective and rigorously provable, even though somewhat
indeterminate.

The probability which our formula assigns, we recall, is a
minimum in two respects, corresponding to the two respects in
which, in the inductive situation, we lack the definite knowledge
of the population required for an exact reckoning. We don't
know the number of the population, so we reckon the probability on that assumption on which the probability is the least
possible, namely, that the number is virtually infinite. We don't
know the composition of the population, so we state the probability which would ensue on the least favorable of all compositions, half-and-half. The point is that even then the resultant
probabilities are satisfactory ones, and comport closely, indeed,
with the degrees of credibility which the most thoughtful in-
quirers have intuitively assigned to the inductions they make.
We can afford to be generous: we have probability to burn.

Some persons may still be dubious just because of the indefiniteness of our results, which hence seem to them somehow
subjective, lacking in logical rigor. Even if the indefiniteness
proves altogether irremediable, however, their delicacy is a
mistake. A somewhat indeterminate logical conclusion like ours
is just as real and objective, just as 'absolute', and just as
rigorously certified, as any could be. It is no less objective and
necessary that the number 6 is greater than 3 (a relatively

indeterminate truth) than that 6 is twice 3 (a more determinate one). If any distinction at all could be made among logical necessities, the former, since it follows '*a fortiori*' from the latter, is more thoroughly necessary, more absolutely rigorous, than the latter. More specifically, we saw on page 42 that the principle of the proportional syllogism provides no less for approximative probabilities like *q is more probable than r*, or *q is very probable*, than for exact ones like *q is probable to the degree $\frac{m}{n}$*.

The argument which we have been pursuing, however, although it stays as close as may be to the beaten path of concepts most likely to be familiar to anyone who has had anything to do with statistical arithmetic, is for the logical philosopher awkward and roundabout, unlikely to fill his bosom with the ardor of living conviction. It has relied, furthermore, on the additive and multiplicative laws which we found a little suspect. There is another way of formulating the solution which may be stated more briefly, which may carry more concrete understanding and confidence, and which puts the probability of an induction directly in terms of one objective ratio of real frequencies and one corresponding proportional syllogism without relying on any ulterior principles. In brief, its principle is this: Any sample, ꭤ, which we may have drawn from a population is itself one of a large class, 𝔐, of possible samples, to wit, the multitude of groups or sets, each of the same size as ꭤ, which are included in the population, and among these the overwhelming majority have the property (𝔓) of matching the population. Hence, by the proportional syllogism, it is overwhelmingly probable that the actual sample ꭤ is one of those which match (𝔓), and hence it is probable that the population matches *it*, that is, has approximately the same composition which we may now discern in the sample.

Consider again, therefore, what we can know *a priori* of any population *M*, consisting of marbles in a bag, stars in the sky, rabbits all over the earth, or anything else, anything whatever. We know in the first place that *M* has some one definite number, and that just one definite proportion of M must have the property P (any property we care to specify, say whiteness). Either all the marbles (or the rabbits or the stars) are white or none is white or half are white or some other fraction between 1 and 0 are white. Now, we know also, *a priori*, by pure logic, that there exist in the population a definite number of smaller groups, sets, or subclasses of any size we care to specify.[2] Thus in a population of 4 marbles there are 6 sets of 2 marbles each — the number of combinations of 4 things taken 2 at a time, $^4C_2$, is 6. With larger populations and with large sets, the number of sets of any specified size is very great — immensely greater, of course, than the number of members of the population. But if the number in the population of individuals (M) is finite, so is the number in any 'hyperpopulation' (𝔐) of sets of any specified size, n, contained in it. There exist, for example, in the total population of marbles, of stars, or of rabbits (or of all three together), just so many sets with 100 members each, so many with 1000 each, so many with 3724, and so forth. Every set, in turn, must contain the specified property P in some one definite proportion — in every set of 100 marbles, or rabbits, for example, either all are white, or none is white, or some intermediate proportion are white. In some of these sets, of the specified size, the proportion of P will be the same, or approximately the same, as the proportion in the original population M: among all the sets of 100 rabbits each which exist in the total rabbit population, some sets will have very nearly the same proportion of white rabbits (20 per cent, 5 per cent, 95 per cent, or whatever it may be) as the whole rabbit population. That is, a certain proportion of the hyper-class (𝔐) of sets must have the property (𝔭) of matching the original population, M. If

---

[2] "Group", "set", and "subclass" are here taken as synonyms. "Group" is perhaps unduly suggestive of 'grouping', as though all the members of any group had to be segregated in one place. That is not intended. What we call "a group" is just a possible selection, a 'combination' in the mathematical sense above defined. "Set" is perhaps the safest and most colorless term.

all M is P or if no M is P, then every set must exactly match. If $\frac{1}{2}$ M is P, the number of matching sets will be the least. But, and this again is the nub of the affair, *whatever* the composition of M with respect to P, more sets will have approximately that composition than any other composition, and if the sets are large, the overwhelming majority of them must have approximately that composition. This too is *a priori*, a law of logic.

Formally, the total number of the hyperpopulation of sets of the size $[MQ]$ which are included in a population M is $^{[M]}C_{[MQ]}$. The number of those sets which contain n Ps and $[MQ] - n$ *non-P*s is $^{[MP]}C_n \times ^{[M\bar{P}]}C_{[MQ]-n}$. The *proportion* of the hyperpopulation which contain n Ps and $[MQ] - n$ *non-P*s is accordingly

$$\frac{^{[MP]}C_n \times ^{[M\bar{P}]}C_{[MQ]-n}}{^{[M]}C_{[MQ]}}.$$

The inductive principle now is the logical law that this proportion is greatest when $\frac{n}{[MQ]}$ is as nearly as possible equal to $\frac{[MP]}{[M]}$, that is, when the composition of the set matches the composition of the population, and that when $[MQ]$ is large (a few hundred, say), the number of the sets in which $\frac{n}{[MQ]}$ is approximately equal to $\frac{[MP]}{[M]}$ is much greater than of all the other sets put together.

There is a difficulty here for the logical imagination because when sets are large enough so that the population-matching sets are in a great majority, there are so many of them that they defy conception except in abstract and symbolic terms. No one can envisage, for example, the whole hyperpopulation of sets of 2500 members each which are embedded right now in a population, say, of 140 million, nor even treat of its number by the resources of common arithmetic. The contemplation of highly simplified examples, however, with conveniently small populations, small sets, and small hyperpopulations of sets, will be of some assistance. In the accompanying diagram is represented *in toto* the hyperpopulation of sets of 3 members each which are contained in a population of 9 (balls, let us say). The number of such sets is given arithmetically by the equation

$$^9C_3 = \frac{9 \times 8 \times 7}{3 \times 2} = 84.$$

Representing the population as divided $\frac{2}{3}$ white and $\frac{1}{3}$ black, the diagram also shows which of the sets are divided in the same proportion and which are not. Arithmetically, the number of sets of 3 members each in which there are 2 white and 1 black (the matching composition) is figured by noting that the subset of 2 white in any such set must be selected from the 6 white in the population, thus providing for $^6C_2$ possibilities, while the subset of 1 black must be chosen from the 3 black in the population, providing for $^3C_1$ possibilities more. Since any one of the white subsets may be conjoined with any one of the black subsets, the total number of matching sets contained in the indicated population is therefore $^6C_2 \times {}^3C_1$, or 15×3, or 45. On the other hand, the number of sets (of 3) in which the composition is the reverse of that of the population, being 1 white and 2 black, is $^6C_1 \times {}^3C_2$, or 6×3, or 18. The number in which all are white is $^6C_3 \times 1$, or 20, and the number in which none is white is $^3C_3$, or 1. Even with so small a selection, we observe, the proportion of matching sets is $\frac{45}{84}$, or 53.5 per cent. This is a large proportion of exact matches, and with so small a group as 3 it is futile to ask for near matches. If we consider now larger sets, we shall find a smaller relative number of exactly matching ones but a greater relative number which either exactly or nearly match. Taking, for example, a population of 24 balls, in which 16 are white, and considering sets of 6, we note that the number of sets which match the population, that is, in which 4 are white and the other 2 non-white, is $^{16}C_4 \times {}^8C_2$, or 1820×28, or 40,960 (already far too many to diagram). The number of sets in which the number of whites is one more than the matching number, i.e., in which the number of whites is 5, is $^{16}C_5 \times {}^8C_1$, or 34,944.

The number of sets in which the number of whites is one too few, namely 3, is $^{16}C_3 \times {}^8C_3$, or 31,360. The total number of sets in which the composition does not vary from the composition of the population by more than one individual, or 16.7 per cent,

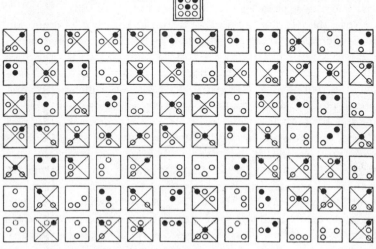

MATCHING SAMPLES

The figure at the top of this diagram represents a population of 9 balls, of which $\frac{1}{3}$ are black and $\frac{2}{3}$ non-black. Each of the 84 squares below it represents one of the samples, sets, or selections, of 3 balls each, which are included in that population. The sets or samples indicated by the check marks are those which have the same composition as the population: that is, each of them is $\frac{1}{3}$ black and $\frac{2}{3}$ non-black. There are 45 — a clear majority — of such matching samples. It is a universal principle, provable by pure arithmetic, that, no matter what the composition of the population, and no matter what the size of the sample, more samples of that size must have (as nearly as possible) the same composition as the population than have any other composition. If the samples are large, then no matter how great the population, the vast majority of them must have approximately the same composition as the population. Given a fair-sized sample, then, from any population, with no further material information, we know logically that it very probably is one of those which match the population, and hence that very probably the population has a composition similar to that which we discern in the sample. This is the logical justification of induction.

therefore, is $40,960 + 34,944 + 31,360$, or $107,264$. The total number of sets of 6 members each which are included in a population of 24 is $^{24}C_6$, or $134,596$. The proportion of those sets which exactly match the population is then only $\frac{40960}{134596}$, or .30, but the proportion of sets which do not differ from the population by more than 16.7 per cent is $\frac{107204}{134596}$, or .80.

Now, the relevance of all this to the justification of induction is plain enough. When we have laid hands or clapped eyes on an inductive sample MQ drawn from a population M, we have chosen one set out of an enormous hyperpopulation of sets or 'protosamples' of the size $[MQ]$ which are included in the population M. Concerning this hyperpopulation there can be proved by pure logic and arithmetic, in a manner suggested though of course not carried through by our elementary formulas and examples, that if the number $[MQ]$ is at all large, the vast majority of protosamples must approximately match the population M with respect to its proportion of the property P, whatever the latter may be. By the ordinary proportional syllogism we were assured that if we know, for example, that the great majority of marbles in a bag are red, it is highly probable that any marble we may draw or have drawn is red. By the same principle, on a higher logical level, since we know *a priori* that the great majority of sets or protosamples which are choosable from a population are statistically similar to that population, it is highly probable that the group which we actually draw as a sample is statistically similar to it, and hence that the population is statistically similar to the sample. Given empirically now that, let us say, $\frac{2}{3}$ of the sample are in fact P, it is highly probable that very nearly $\frac{2}{3}$ of the population are P. Without knowing exactly the size and composition of the original population to begin with, we cannot calculate, as in the artificial examples of the preceding paragraphs, exactly what proportion of our 'hyper-marbles' have the quality of nearly-matching-the-population, but we do know *a priori* that most of them have it. Before we choose one of them, it is hence very probable that the one we choose will be one of those which match or nearly match;

after we have chosen one, it remains highly probable that the population closely matches the one we have, so that we need only look at the one we have to read off what the population, probably and approximately, is like.

Every sample, in other words, is like a chip, marked with a fractional number, drawn from a bucket of chips among which we know most of the chips are marked with the true composition of the population in which we are interested. It is by thus treating the whole sample *MQ* as a single chip or counter or hyper-marble in a bagful of the same that we have been able to formulate the validity of induction in terms of one straightforward syllogistic probability instead of by the enormous combination of probabilities to which we resorted in an earlier part of this chapter. The fact that such a redaction is possible will bring home forcibly to the student who has read elsewhere on these subjects that our result is a plain 'direct' probability, and not an 'inverse' probability of the kind usually appealed to by theories which employ the laws of large numbers to justify induction, and that it accordingly does not require the questionable assumption, utilized by the latter, that the moot population is antecedently as likely to have one composition as another. It does, to be sure, presuppose that any one sample, or chip, or counter, is antecedently as likely to be selected as any other, or at any rate that there is no evidence that the principle of selection is relevant to the quality of the sample, but this, as we observed in Chapter 3 and shall observe again in Chapter 6, is an innocent truism.

Although we have now avoided the complication of probabilities which we earlier employed, our new probability is in fact, of course, equal to the probability yielded before, and its calculation must proceed by similar mathematical steps. It has accordingly the same kind of indeterminateness as our previous results. We cannot assert exactly what proportion of protosamples match the population. We know, however, that if they are large, most of them do; we know that the proportion of matching is the least when the population is virtually infinite

and is divided half and half. We know how great is the pre-
ponderance of matching protosamples, of any specified size,
under these worst possible conditions, and hence can assert
what is the least possible probability that a sample of a given
size will match to any specified degree of approximation. All
this can be read off again, nearly enough, from the formula for
the standard error of sampling, and from the supplementary
tables, and is indeed the way in which the formula is commonly
explained in statistical texts. The fact that with a sample of
2500, σ equals or is less than .01, may be now interpreted to mean
that of all the possible samples of 2500 members apiece which
are included in any given population, the proportion which
match the sample within 1 per cent must be *at least* .6826, while
the proportion which match within 2 per cent cannot be less
than .9545, and so forth.

At the beginning of this chapter, we desiderated as 'the inductive principle', adequate to justify induction, the proposition that any sizable sample very probably matches its population in any specifiable respect. We have provided this, and
more, by the more exact and definite sampling formula,

$$\vdash : \sigma \gtreqless \frac{.5}{\sqrt{[MQ]}},$$

which we now interpret to mean that the proportion of samples
that match within the margin expressed by the right-hand term
cannot be less than .6826, and so forth. To make perfectly plain,
however, the manner in which any particular induction is to be
reduced to a proportional syllogism of the form made familiar by
our Chapter 2, we must acquire a major premise of the familiar
form by logically 'specifying' the sampling law by supplying the
numbers discoverable in the case in question. We shall then
have, for example: *At least 68 per cent of the sets of 2500 members
each which are included in the population of rabbits do not vary in
composition from the population itself by more than .01.* From the
data we obtain the minor premise, *The observed sample is a set
of 2500 members included in the population of rabbits.* Thus there

follows, with a probability of at least .68, *The observed sample does not differ in composition from the population by more than .01*, or, what is equivalent, *The composition of the rabbit population is equal to a quantity between 1 per cent less than the composition of the sample and 1 per cent greater than it.* From the data now we supply the value .20, let us say, for *the composition of the sample*. Simple arithmetic then furnishes the final answer, with the indicated probability: *The composition of the rabbit population lies between .19 and .21.*

I have persistently repeated, with numerous minor variations, the main topics of our argument, and have labored the simple arithmetical steps which it needs, for the benefit of readers unaccustomed to the arithmetical theory of classes, who may be suddenly illumined by one turn of phrase where they have been stubbornly opaque to others. The actual process of making inductions is extraordinarily familiar to us, while the manner of thought required for its abstract justification, though simple and fundamental in principle, is off the beaten track of our ordinary discourse. In particular, it is hard for most of us to keep in mind without confusion the various interlocking and overlapping classes, and classes of classes, and their arithmetical ratios, which the scheme involves. We must distinguish: the population M, and the proportion of P in M, which is the object of our inductive quest; the actual sample MQ, and the proportion of P in MQ, which is the datum of our induction; and the hyper-population, $ℍ_{[MQ]}$, of groups of the size $[MQ]$ which are included in M, and the proportion of this hyperpopulation which match the population M with respect to the proportion in which they evince the character P. In our diagram a few pages back, the population M is represented by the single figure at the top; the hyperpopulation of groups or sets (protosamples) of 3 which are included in M is represented by the rest of the figure.[3]

---

[3] Logically, the groups or sets are *members* of the hyperpopulation $ℍ$, which is a class of classes. They are not members of, but are subclasses or species logically included in, the population M.

The cardinal syllogism on which hinges the validity of an inductive inference, though cogent in exactly the same way as any other proportional syllogism, is peculiar in certain respects which may be distracting. (1) Its reference class 𝕸 is a class of classes, and the major premise is accordingly a statistical proposition of the second level. (2) Its major term 𝕻 is an oddly relational property of classes, namely, (a) 'matching the population' (whatever the latter may be), (b) within a certain range of approximation. (3) The composition of 𝕸 with respect to 𝕻 is not statable exactly but only approximately — 'at least .95', etc. (4) The major premise is analytic and a priori, a principle of the logic and arithmetic of classes, or a specification thereof.

None of these oddities militates against the validity of the inductive syllogism. In the respects which are relevant to the syllogism, a character like 'approximately matching the population' behaves exactly like the simple quality red, for example. The margin of indeterminateness in assigning the composition of 𝕸 and the consequent probability is a trait which the inductive syllogism shares with many others. The analytic necessity of the major premise is just what the validity of induction requires if it is not to rest, circle-wise and futilely, on induction itself. Although as a principle of logic, or an exemplification of one, the supreme premise need not be expressed, any more than the principle of Barbara need be stated in a valid demonstrative syllogism, but may be thought of as simply the principle of inference by which we pass from the other premise to the conclusion, nevertheless it perfectly well may be expressed. It is true, and the conclusion follows validly from it, and by expressing it we achieve what we set out to accomplish, a clear proof that an induction has a high degree of the kind of credibility which is yielded by a proportional syllogism at its best.

The cardinal principle that most of the possible samples selectable from any population must statistically match the population, in any assignable respect, naturally is nothing new, for all that it has been so much ignored by philosophical logicians and so seldom expressed and utilized in the way which we have just carried through. Works on probability and statistics abound with *a priori* laws of large numbers which are varied editions of it. In using the principle we have been content to take it in its narrowest form, as it applies one by one to any given population and a certain sized sample thereof. We can in fact, of course, say more: that of *all* largish samples, of mixed sizes, contained in any population, the vastly larger number match the population in the stipulated respect; and indeed that in the whole stupendous hyper-class consisting of all the combinations of populations, sets, and predicate properties in the world, that is, the hyper-class each of whose members consists of one population, one set from that population, and one property P, the overwhelming majority are such that the 'set' matches the population with respect to the property.[4] Whenever we fix upon any one triad of population, sample, and predicate, therefore, it is highly probable that what we have is one of the matching sets. There is some value in reflecting on such statistical vastitudes in order to appreciate how the validity and success of induction are only the glittering iceberg-tip of an all-pervasive and inevitable logical marshaling of the universe. They are cumbersome, however, and unnecessary to our argument, which proceeds more simply and determinately by confining attention to the rules establishing a definite statistical relation among just the populations, samples, and predicates with which we may deal. We can continue to speak of 'a sample' matching 'its population' because, although every set, of course, is a sample of innumerable populations, in innumerable respects, we suppose 'the' population and 'the' respect in question to be stipulated along with the selection of the sample.

Our incorporation of the logical law of large numbers into a sort of inductive syllogism makes plain how an induction satisfies what is perhaps the most convincing prescription for an

---

[4] Purists will be pleased to emend this statement to restrict its generality, so that the idea of 'all populations' shall not incur the paradoxes of the idea of the class of all classes. We can cope well enough with all populations whose members are low-level individuals.

inference with a high degree of logical credibility, namely, that it belong to a class of possible inferences in which the great majority of those with true premises have true conclusions. The composition of every protosample included in any population provides a true possible premise for an inductive inference to the conclusion that the composition of the population is approximately the same, and the conclusions of most of those inferences necessarily are true. Any actual inference, from an observed sample, is a realization of one of those possible inferences, and hence very probably has a true conclusion. *Quod erat demonstrandum.*

5

THE LOGIC OF SCIENCE

The crucial part of our task has been done. We have made clear to ourselves how a certain variety of classic probabilities are genuinely degrees of the same brand of credibility which is furnished by a logical entailment, and how an inductive inference from the composition of a sample to the composition of its population has that kind of logical credibility in a high degree.

We may leave it to mathematicians and logisticians to fill in the sketchy outline of our proof, in full generality, with the fit equations and with the compact train of symbolic derivations which we have scamped. It is for us here rather to round out our accomplishment philosophically by noting, in the merely semi-technical vein which we have been pursuing, how when once the validity of straightforward sampling is established, the whole roster of principles of empirical or scientific inference may be expected to fall into place, proved and organized in the one logic. All the *forms* of inference commonly called 'inductive' would thus be accommodated, and the forms would be demonstrably applicable to every *kind* of problem and subject matter.

The inductive form which has been most earnestly practiced and contemplated by philosophers and logicians, frequently to the exclusion of all the rest of the spectrum, is 'universal' induction, from the datum that *all MQ is P* to the conclusion that all *M* is *P*. Universal generalizations of this sort, and the corresponding negative, *No M is P*, deserve some of their special reputation because they are in principle completely determinate in a manner in which intermediate proportional laws are not. Knowing that all *M* is *P*, or no *M* is *P*, we know not only the composition of *M* with respect to *P*, that is, the proportion of *P*s among the *M*s, but also its 'constitution', the actual allotment of *P* or of *non-P* to every individual member of *M*. Hence comes the difference in effectiveness between the universal syllogisms, Barbara and Celarent, which give categorical conclusions concerning any individual class member or any subclass covered by the middle term, and the proportional syllogisms which give only intermediate probabilities. As an instrument for anticipating life's emergencies, the universal generalization is consequently much more valuable. So far as concerns inductive confirmation, however, universal conclusions are not set apart from the rest, and they inevitably lose in their confirmation the fine edge of their ideal perfection, though they are still the most valuable kind of generalization. We infer from *100 per cent of MQ is P* to *100 per cent of M is P* with the same sort of warrant with which we infer from *63 per cent of MQ is P* to *63 per cent of M is P*, and so we can draw either conclusion only probably and approximately. We know, to be sure, that if all *M* is *P*, then exactly all *MQ* is certain to be *P*´(as we do not know that if 63 per cent of *M* is *P*, exactly 63 per cent of *MQ* must be *P*), but the converse does not follow. Inductively, on our present scheme, we know only that if all of 2500 *MQ*s are *P*, for example, there is a probability of at least .95 that not less than 98 per cent of *M* is *P*. If we are to have a greater logical confidence than this, or a closer approximation, it must come from a larger sample or from subsidiary sources which we examine hereafter, and we can never quite touch either exactness or certitude. This leaves unaffected all the real significance of universal laws for thought and action, but it lays bare the serious confusion in the too common notion, to be found even among philosophical scientists, that science promises certainty if and only if it discovers universal laws (as the older scientists expected) and not merely proportional laws (as the newer science suspects). Since completely universal laws, where they exist, could be known by empirical methods only probably and approximately, science could not give certainty in either event, and any possible effect on the credibility of the single case, *a is P*, of the difference between a universal and a nearly universal law is swallowed up in the margin of inductive probability anyhow. The confusion has been much encouraged by the custom of using the phrase "probability law", which is properly applied to the logical principles of probability, to mean indifferently two other things: *law which is known only with probability* (which characterizes all natural laws) and *law from which only a probability can be known* (the peculiarity of merely statistical laws). The latter use is reminiscent of the vulgar error that 'the laws of probability' govern dice throws. The whole difficulty suggests a lingering belief, in an unlikely quarter, in the traditional idea that for a proposition to be *universal* is for it to be *necessary* and apodeictically certain.

As against both those who would suppose that all universal laws must be logically necessary and those who deny that there are any universal natural laws, it is pertinent to point out that there must exist universal laws in nature, of a quite contingent sort, even though they be of less caliber and importance than enthusiasts for the uniformity of nature have sometimes hoped. For any two characters, M and P, must be connected by either a universal or a merely proportional law. If they are connected by a merely proportional law, say that 62 per cent of M is P, then the 62 per cent constitute a subclass of M, say MT, and *all MT is P*. Furthermore, at the other extreme, we can count as individuals of a new class, U, any congeries of, say, 10,000 Ms, and as a new predicate, W, the 'complexion' of such a congeries when it contains about 62 per cent P. It follows by our law of large numbers that at any rate *nearly all U is W*, and as we consider larger congeries as members of U, the proportion of U which is W will differ from 1 by an amount less than any quantity, however small, which we care to assign — certainly less than the margin of inductive approximation. Since the macroscopic objects of our daily traffic are in sooth congeries of many trillions of elemental particles or events, any sort of proportional laws holding among the latter will generate some virtually categorical laws among the former.[1]

The M and P of the inductive conclusion may be of any complexity; in particular, they may be complex relational properties. Thus we may infer from an appropriate sample that all the husbands of ingenue moving-picture actresses are followers of the races. With this variation the principle of universal generalization suffices to establish the causal laws which bulk so large in common-sense experience and in the simpler results of science. Whatever else a causal connection may involve, say the connection between heating a piece of wood and its catching fire, the necessary and sufficient condition of our use of the connection for prediction or control is that there shall be a law that whenever M (heating a piece of wood to a certain temperature, for example) occurs, then P (the ignition of the wood, for example) occurs. This is a universal law, *All M is P*, with only some slight complication to accommodate the notion that cause and effect may be distinguishable events, adjacent and successive: For every x which is a piece of wood to which a certain degree of heat is applied, there is a y, adjacent and successive to x, such that y is burning wood. A stricter or reciprocating causal law, that when and only when M occurs, P occurs, is composed of a complementary pair of universal laws, *All M is P and all P is M*. Most of the causal laws in ordinary use are conditioned: under certain conditions, say 'normal' conditions, P occurs when and only when M occurs — *All NM is P and all NP is M*. These are inducible in essentially the same way as the simpler sort.

We can judge from the above how nearly right are such hal-

---

[1] To be exact, the proposition expressed by this last sentence follows from the preceding, which is logically necessary, only with a very high probability. Our macroscopic objects are only a selection from the total hyperpopulation of congeries and it is only highly probable, and not certain, that the chances will mature with respect to them.

lowed formulas as that universal induction proceeds 'from the less general to the more general' and 'from the particular to the general' ('from some to all'). That is, universal induction proceeds from a proposition about *all* of a species MQ to a proposition about all of its genus M, but it requires, in addition to the universal premise that all MQ is P (that there is no $MQ\bar{P}$) the particular or existential premise that there are n members of MQP. As logicians have long pointed out, neither *All MQ is P* nor *All M is P* entails that there are any Ms. The reason that common sense always assumes, when it accepts a law *All M is P*, that there are Ms, is that a material law worth asserting has been induced from premises which do include a definite existential statement about some Ms.

It may perhaps go without saying now that if simple universal and proportional laws can be validly induced, so can all the more complex parameters characteristic of the empirical sciences. Functional laws, ranging from the terrestrial law of falling bodies, $v = 32t$, to the most recondite equations of contemporary physics, are establishable by the same sampling logic as simple *All M is P*. If all observed falling bodies at the earth's surface have had a velocity in feet per second equal to 32 times the interval of fall, in seconds, then probably all falling bodies at the earth's surface share that complex property. The induction of statistical averages and correlations can safely proceed on the ground that they are all derivable from frequency distributions which in turn are constituted by sets of proportional laws, and the latter can be induced singly or together like any proportional laws. Statisticians have long employed variations of the σ formula to yield directly the probable approximation of inductions concerning any of these quantities, and that usage, as well as more delicate methods latterly applied to problems of estimation and significance, along with all the complex lore of curve-fitting, is justifiable with sufficient accuracy when once the epistemological jam is broken by a valid philosophy of sampling.

We have still, however, been exclusively occupied with the induction of generalities, either universal or proportional, and I

have written as though, when we infer from the observed part
of the class M to some further member of M, say a, we must
first infer to a general proposition concerning the composition
of the whole class M and then infer syllogistically to the nature
of a. Psychologically this is certainly not true to our mental
processes, which proceed from the observed M to the next member a without detouring via generalities concerning all M. This
procedure, which we noticed in Chapter 1 as a 'telescoped' form
of inference, was the one kind in which Hume was interested.
It has no one good name, but has been variously called "inference from particulars to particulars" (J. S. Mill), "inference
from singulars to singulars" (C. D. Broad), "inductive correlation" (J. M. Keynes), "succession" (Venn), "eduction"
(Johnson and Broad), "prediction" (R. Carnap). Patently,
now, if the sample gives a probability of p that the relative frequency of P in M (or in $M\overline{Q}$) is q, then it gives a probability of
at least p $\times$ q that an a which is $M\overline{Q}$ is P. Just as patently,
however, it gives a much higher probability, because q is only
the most probable frequency and p is only *its* probability.
There are other probabilities, some of them almost as large, for
other frequencies, some of *them* larger (unless q = 1), and the
net total probability that a is P is the sum of the products of
all these values. The upshot of it all is a logical justification
of the ordinary assumption of enlightened common sense and of
the scientists that if MQ is fairly large, the probability that any
further member of M will be P is nearly equal to the relative
frequency of P in MQ. If I have encountered 200 wire-haired
terriers, for example, and 85 per cent of them have tried to bite
me, the probability that the next will try is so close to .85 that
the discrepancy is negligible; if all have tried to bite me, it is
not certain that the next will try, but it is nearly certain —
much more nearly certain than that all the rest will try. There
must be emphasized, however, that in spite of the fact that the
inductive probability that an a which is M but not a member of
the observed set MQ will be P is approximately the same in
degree as the deductive probability that a b which *is* a member

of MQ is P, the two are profoundly different in principle, with one of the deepest of philosophical gaps, the problem of induction, between them.

This principle of 'prediction' lets us infer from the perceived to the unperceived in as much as it lets us infer that a, which we have perceived to be M but not perceived to be P, *is P.* It also however lets us infer the existence of an object b with a property M, even though we have not perceived it at all, and this is the main method by which our knowledge widens out circle by circle from the little patch of daily experience to the wide ambit of the universe. The extension requires only the kind of relational version of inductive generalization witnessed in connection with causal inference above. Expanding the affair to the syllogistic form, we require for inferring that there is an unobserved y with the property M the major premise, *For every object or event x, if x has a property N, there exists a y to which x has the relation R* (bigger than it, adjacent to it, preceding it, twenty miles to the northwest of it, or what not) *and which has the property M;* more shortly, '*Every N is R to an M*'. Given then an a which is N we can infer that there is a b which is M even though we cannot observe it. This is the principle on which, inducing that wherever there are a watch dial and case there are wheels sandwiched between, I infer from observing my watch dial and case that there are wheels inside. The proof of the major premise is an ordinary enough induction: the complex predicate *being R to an M* behaves logically like any inductive predicate P. The usefulness of the proposition depends on our being able to observe an N without observing whether it is R to an M (able, for example, to observe a watch case without observing either that it does or that it does not enclose a set of wheels). The possibility of confirming it, on the other hand, depends on our being able to observe of some Ns whether they are R to Ms and on our observing in fact that all or most of these are R to Ms; it depends, for example, on our being able to observe of some watch cases whether they contain wheels, and on our discovery that all of those cases do contain wheels. These characters are not really peculiar, however, for the value of every induction depends similarly on the fact that the sample MQ consists, not of all the things observed to be M, but of all the things observed to be M and *also* observed with respect to whether they are P. Swans, stars, microbes, and so forth — these have always been discoverable in connection with certain kinds of circumstances, and the occurrence of those circumstances now, or other circumstances which promise the occurrence of those circumstances, is inductive warrant that there are more and more swans, stars, and microbes. Even for a class of objects which are never observed — electrons, say — the inductive method will work, because though just that complex of characters is never observed, instances of its components have been observed; otherwise we couldn't conceive the combination. If we know inductively the conditions under which the components occur, we know the complex of conditions under which the compound occurs.

The inductive principle can provide also the foundations of what is called 'diagnosis', 'presumption of fact', or simply 'hypothesis' — the confirmation of a proposition, usually a singular one, by the verification of its consequents. Thus Einstein's theory of relativity was confirmed by observing that the mass of the sun deflected rays of light in the manner deducible from the theory, and so forth; thus the detective decides that Harold Harbinger committed the crime because all the evidence is exactly what one would expect on the supposition that he did. This kind of inference, taken in its purest form, with none of the auxiliaries usually combined with it, may be construed as carried by the principles that if and only if all the consequents of a hypothesis are true, the hypothesis is true, while if all its tested consequents have been proved true, then probably all its consequents are true, and so accordingly is the hypothesis.

Hypothesis thus understood as a universal generalization concerning all the properties which belong to a given individual is logically the counterpart of ordinary induction, which is a universal generalization concerning all the individuals which have a certain property. Pure argument by 'analogy' — though pure analogy is a rare procedure — is related to hypothesis in the same way as argument from particulars to particulars is related to ordinary inductive generalization: it consists in inferring that since all or most of the observed properties of an object, or all its properties of a certain kind, are shared by another object, a specified further property of the first object is probably shared by the second. If your house, for example, is built by the same contractor as mine, on a similar plan and with similar materials, and mine has proved reasonably weathertight, there is reason by analogy to expect yours to be so too.

For various reasons it is perhaps less common to confirm hypotheses on the simple inductive plan which we have considered than by the process epitomized in one of the formulas referred to as 'Bayes' theorem' or the principle of 'inverse probability'. This principle is easily derivable from the multiplicative law as we gave it on page 48. Omitting the left-hand "qr/p" in the equation there, we have

$$(1) \vdash: q/p \times r/pq = r/p \times q/pr.$$

Dividing both sides of this equation by q/p, we have

$$(2) \vdash: r/pq = \frac{r/p \times q/pr}{q/p}.$$

This is Bayes' theorem, or one version of it. It is a wholly general law of probability concerning the relations of any three propositions, but its most popular use is as a rule for the confirmation of a hypothesis r by a new datum q in conjunction with previous knowledge p. It means then that the probability of the hypothesis r in relation to the two batches of evidence, p and q, is directly proportioned to the antecedent probability of the hypothesis (its probability in relation to the old knowledge p) and to its explanatory force (the probability with which the datum q can be 'predicted' from the hypothesis r in conjunction with the old knowledge p), and is inversely proportioned to the antecedent probability of the datum (that is, to the probability with which the datum was predictable from previous knowledge alone, irrespective of the hypothesis r). Given, for example, (p) a good deal of general knowledge about a murder and about our suspect, Harold Harbinger, plus the clue (q) that his knife was found near the scene of the crime, the net eventual probability that Harbinger is guilty (r) is equal to the quotient:

$$\frac{\text{(The antecedent probability} \times \text{(The probability that if Harbinger}}{\text{that Harbinger would do it)}\ \ \ \text{did it he would leave his knife)}}{\text{(The probability that his knife would be there anyhow)}}.$$

The appearance of the quantity q/pr in this rule exhibits the justification of the notion that a hypothesis is confirmed by the verifying of a consequent q, but makes clear at the same time that the hypothesis does not ordinarily, all by itself, predict a piece of evidence q, but does so in conjunction with other knowledge p, assumed as the context of the particular investigation, and even then does not often entail q with certainty but only with some degree of probability. The theorem too is like the multiplicative law in being incapable of providing fundamental probabilities: all the component probabilities which it demands (r/p, q/p, q/pr) can and must eventually be supplied by the results of previous inductive sampling.

Singular propositions, however, are less often confirmed either by a direct induction of properties or by the rule of Bayes than logicians and scientists allege, but are deduced by statistical syllogism or induced by the foreshortened argument from particulars to particulars. Thus I believe that Johnny has measles, not because I have found the consequents of that hypothesis to accord with his symptoms, but because he has certain symptoms of which I know, from previous induction, that 98 per cent of those who have them have measles. Sherlock Holmes then was not so mistaken after all when he invoked 'the science of deduction'.

With Bayes' theorem we broach the great store of probability principles which are familiar to students of the traditional calculus. There remains outstanding only one theoretical need of our probability logic which is controversial enough to consider separately, the need for a 'cumulative principle'. Bayes' theorem gives us a formula for computing the probability of any one proposition r in relation to any conjunction of two propositions, p and q. This is the converse of what is given by the multiplicative law, i.e., the probability of any conjunction of propositions, qr, in relation to any one proposition p. The multiplicative law, however, at least when q and r are independent, produces its results from facts concerning just the separate probabilities of q and r in relation to p. To maintain the parallel, we should have now to produce the probability r/pq from facts concerning just the separate probabilities of r in relation to p and to q. Bayes' theorem does not manage this; it does utilize r/p, but it does not use r/q, and it requires knowledge of the strange cross-connections, q/pr and q/p. What we call a 'cumulative law' would let us compute the cumulative probability r/pq from r/p and r/q. Its usefulness, if not its indispensability, is recognized when we remember that a given proposition r will generally have different probabilities in relation to different propositions ('bodies of evidence') p and q, and still a different probability in relation to the conjunction pq. One would expect that no probability operation would be more natural and necessary than the cumulation of a proposition's probability in relation to all the evidence together, from its probabilities in relation to the successive data separately. Actually, however, hardly any topic in the philosophy of probability is so surrounded by obscurity and dissent. One promising formula in favor with older writers has been the simple classical theorem for reckoning the effect of witnesses' testimony. Appropriately edited, this gives us that

$$r/pq = \frac{r/p \times r/q}{(r/p \times r/q) + (\sim r/p \times \sim r/q)},$$

where "$\sim r$" stands for *not-r*, the denial or negation of r, its probability being equal to 1 minus the probability of r. This rule seems to require considerably more generous allowances than the multiplicative law. We need not enter the debate over it since it affects only the detail of the logic of probability and, although a useful auxiliary to the inductive principle, is not at all presupposed by it.

Given our principle of sampling, augmented by such methods of compounding probabilities from different sources as Bayes' theorem and perhaps some more direct cumulative principle, we may look forward to unraveling, codifying, and correcting the whole logic of empirical inquiry, not only the standard 'procedures' of scientific research and the rules of juridical evidence which experts in these departments have implicitly recognized, usually with surprising vagueness and indecision, but such logicians' and philosophers' formulas as Mill's canons, Peirce's rule of 'predesignation', and the rules of '*Prüfbarkeit*' and confirmation of more recent authors. In this process we should disclose how the same concept of probability is univocally applicable, not merely in principle but in practice, to the whole range of uncertain knowledge, from the guesses of the gamester and the actuary to the soberest conjecture of the historian or the ontologist. Since the one probability concept is fundamentally statistical, all these credibilities will be essentially quantitied and measurable. We don't often remember, to be sure, how many MQ we have observed, nor even exactly what proportion of them have been P, and we seldom work through the calculations required for establishing an exact probability even when we have the fundamental statistics. To that extent our actual results will have a fringe of indeterminateness or will consist of a mere vague impression of 'very likely' or 'out of the question'. This however is no more than the fact that we seldom exactly measure any of the measurable aspects of the world, and it no more militates against the measurability of credibility than the fact that I have never taken the trouble to measure my child's swing deprives it of a definite height. Our philosophy accordingly confirms and is confirmed by the age-old readiness of shrewd men to *bet* at agreed numerical odds on the results either of a dice game or of a presidential election — a propensity not easily explicable in the categories of those theories of credibility which deny that it is measurable.

By means of the coöperation of probability principles, not only hypothesis and analogy but inductive generalization itself may be greatly refined and fortified, far beyond the nuclear probabilities obtainable by simple sampling, or, according to circumstances, much reduced below that figure. A universal generalization, for instance, given a certain number of data, i.e., a certain sized sample, may still be more or less probable according as its scope is narrower or wider, as the data on which it is based are known to be similar or dissimilar in many respects to the rest of the objects which it covers, and as the data are known to be otherwise dissimilar or similar to one another. A diagnostic hypothesis is similarly advantaged (or conversely disadvantaged) in a logical way in so far as it is economical or parsimonious and its confirmatory data are not only numerous but various. A statistical or non-universal generalization is probable, again, in proportion as the sample can be known to be statistically similar to the population in other respects than those covered by the generalization (M and P). *A posteriori*, the results of previous inductions contribute to, or detract from, the probability of new generalizations or hypotheses. A proposed universal or statistical generalization, or a diagnostic hypothesis, for instance, may have a high probability irrespective of its sample, provided that it follows from some more general principle already well established in similar areas, or it may have a low probability, in the teeth of abundant instances, because it conflicts with such a well established general principle. Most arguments by 'analogy' depend almost wholly on previous inductions which show that the similarity between datum and object is relevant to the character in question. If we infer that the Earth and Mars are sufficiently similar to make it likely that life, which is known to occur on Earth, occurs also on Mars, we do not just blindly count resemblances. We rely on the law, established by terrestrial generalization, that certain conditions are necessary and sufficient for the occurrence of life, and we then find in Mars' possession of these conditions the syllogistic minor premise which enables the conclusion that it supports life.

Even when previous inductive experience does not by itself give a direct clue to the truth or falsity of a proposed new inductive conclusion, it may greatly facilitate the latter by decreeing what kind of sample is especially likely to be representative. In what we called 'derivative induction' on page 9, our store of inductive knowledge is sufficient so that a single instance of a new induction, properly selected, is enough to give it a very high probability, as when a single observation of the plumage changes of a newly discovered bird species is taken to be authoritative for the whole species. A similar result follows more laboriously where what are called 'Mill's methods' of causal induction are applicable. When experience has persuaded us that the universal causal accompaniment of a certain character must reside among a relatively small set of alternatives, then a single further instance may eliminate all but one of these, either because the character is present in it without them or because they are present without the character. In a less wholesale manner, accumulated knowledge may indicate that certain kinds of samples, or samples collected according to certain prescriptions, are at any rate more likely to be representative than others. If all MQ is P, the additional knowledge that the properties peculiar to the sample, namely, the components of Q, are generally inimical to P (are negatively associated with P), increases the resultant probability that all M is P, while knowledge that Q is generally favorable to P (is positively associated with it) very much reduces the probability.

The conditions under which statistical samples are particularly effective, or particularly ineffective, have become, thanks to the public opinion polls, a veritable part of our folklore. Thus we know that a statistical generalization is more probable according as its parameter remains stable as the sample is enlarged, or is the same in several independently chosen samples. A single sample, we know, is more effective if it is 'stratified' in a manner similar to that of the population, that is, if it possesses in the same ratios as the population the sundry properties which are known, by previous inductions, to be relevant, or likely to be relevant, to the predicate under investigation, and is correspondingly unreliable as this symmetry is violated, as when presidential straw votes are collected from predominantly well-to-do citizens. When stratification is impractical, statistical samples may be chosen by a so-called 'random' method, by a lottery, for example, which a wide empirical knowledge of causal and statistical connections indicates is especially unlikely to load the evidence one way or the other.

Buoying up many kinds of inductions are two especially wide and primitive inductive generalizations: that the world is on the whole remarkably regular or 'uniform' and remarkably continuous. The uniformity of nature, consisting in the fact that a gratifyingly large proportion of the pairs of the prominent or important characters are universally connected, gives a boost to any proposed universal generalization of certain broadly identifiable varieties. The more general law of statistical regularity, the empirical law of large numbers, boosts every generalization whatever, universal or proportional. Whereas the logical law of large numbers, we remember, is that the great majority of the subclasses of any class must be statistically similar to each other and to the class, the empirical law (in its inductive application) is that in observed fact the subclasses which we select as samples are customarily, as we should expect, among those that match each other and the populations which we take them to exemplify. Inductive probabilities, in other words, have so far been in the habit of maturing. The antecedent logical probability that a given sample is representative, therefore, is increased by the fact that our samples generally have been representative. The 'continuity' of the world may be understood as a sort of special regularity of events with respect to space and time: except for some recent indications concerning the ultimate quantum of action, experience has steadily revealed that objects commonly remain in the same states, in most respects, for considerable periods, and that when they change, either in quality or in location, they change gradually and continuously. Closely akin to the discovery both of regularity and of continuity is the discovery of concrete things and natural kinds — the prevalence of bundles of properties which (*a*) endure, or change gradually, and (*b*) are regularly associated with one another. Most of the objects of our inductions are already known to be members of natural kinds — stoves, stars, men — and so to be especially fertile of universal connections.

The inductions of science, finally, are advantaged by the broad discovery that the laws of the world are not single and isolated but compose hierarchical systems, laws of different logical dimensions, and laws from which other laws are deducible. Functional laws are properly impressive because of their higher dimension of regularity and continuity: $v = 32t$ is a generalization covering not only all instances of any one velocity and time of fall, say 224 feet per second and 7 seconds, but all velocities and all times of fall. It means, furthermore, not merely that every velocity is perfectly associated with a time (i.e., that there is a perfect statistical 'contingency' between velocity and time) but that velocities and times are continuously associated in such wise that if a velocity v_2 lies between two velocities, v_1 and v_3, then the time t_2 which is associated with v_2 lies between the times, t_1 and t_3, which are associated respectively with v_1 and v_3 (there is a perfect 'correlation' between velocity and time of fall). Another kind of hierarchy and nesting of laws, either qualitative or functional, results from the fact that the components of complex objects are less varied than the objects themselves, and the many laws which govern the behavior of the objects may be deduced from the few laws which govern the behavior of their components. As we delve deeper, explore more widely, analyze more closely, we always discover — leaving aside for the moment certain jigsaw puzzles of quantum theory — more regularity, continuity, and hierarchy, laws within laws like Chinese boxes, more general laws entailing and explaining less general, as the forms of gravitation bind logically the laws of planetary action, falling apples, and artillery practice.

The caroming of a billiard ball would be inductively predictable after a few observations even if it were an unusual, isolated, and discontinuous kind of event, devoid of analytic insides and systematic context. Given, however, the results of that immense fabric of inductions, stretching from the spin of the electron to the parade of the galaxies, which surrounds and supports our beliefs concerning the billiard ball's behavior, the convergent force of the evidence as well as the psychological sense of inevitability is multiplied. So wrong is it to object to our doctrine of induction that 'the world is not like a bag of marbles' that our rule can in this way work far more effectively with the world populations involved in concrete research than with the idealized set of loose marbles by which we have previously illustrated it.

So solid and enormous is the storied bulk of knowledge and experience which frames every inductive conclusion today, so sure are we that no matter how unlike two processes appear it's a good bet that if we delve into them we'll find the same parts and principles at work in both, and so accustomed are we to finding a 'reason', in the form of a wider law or a more detailed circumstance, for every flat visible concomitance of qualities, that it is easy to forget the principal and original rôle of inductive probabilities altogether. The philosophic tyro or traditionalist is hence easily persuaded that natural laws are more than statistical concomitances and are discoverable by another method than sampling. Philosophical logicians from Aristotle to John Dewey have distinguished 'essential', 'abstract', or 'specific' universal propositions from 'accidental', 'collective', or 'enumerative' ones — the former being supposed to embody an inner and necessary connection between subject M and predicate P whilst the latter are mere statistical concomitances. Thus the idealists imagine that all we need in order to find the real scientific truth is a kind of organic insight. Even the natural scientist, who by this time can expect every new functional generalization to be either a specialization or a generalization of regularities already familiar, joins the schoolmen and the Hegelians in fancying that careful observation of a single instance is enough to warrant his conclusions and that if he resorts to plural observations it is only to diminish the danger that he is in error in his comprehension of the one instance. Eminent researchers express disdain for inductive generalization as a scientific method, and writers on the subject periodically repeat Bacon's ungrateful verdict that enumerative induction is 'puerile'.

These pretensions, I am sure, are mistaken, but they are sincere tributes to the power of inductive sampling to create convictions so strong as to ape necessity and self-evidence. There doubtless are 'essential' propositions, necessarily true 'by definition', like *All parrots are birds* — the laws of logic are among them — but the laws of natural science certainly are not of that variety. The fact that one scientific law can be deduced from another does nothing to prove either of them intrinsically necessary. When the idealistic logician illustrates the distinction between a 'real' law and a 'mere factual concomitance' by contrasting, as a mere concomitance, *Eating arsenic is followed by death* with the 'deeper' laws which explain that concomitance, *Arsenic hardens tissues* and *Hardened tissues are fatal,*[2] it is not hard to see that he now has two factual concomitances instead of the original one and that he would reach nothing but factual concomitances, though he might attain considerable systematic economy, if he traced the succession back to some first principles of nature. If his explanatory principles had been really necessary, the vulgar local law deducible from them would have had to be necessary too.

It is no detriment to a law that it is not necessary: all the valuable consequents of a law, necessary or contingent, follow

[2] The example is from *Logic Deductive and Inductive* (New York, 1896, 1905, and 1923; page 188) by J. G. Hibben, who cites Bosanquet and others as holding the same opinion on the subject.

from the bare fact that all M is P, which is common to both kinds. The fact that the principles of natural science are contingent concomitances, however, or if they are necessary are necessary in such an occult way that we cannot directly perceive their necessity, does mean that they must be confirmed eventually by inductive sampling — that the whole august pyramid of knowledge, of law and counter-law, must rest on the plebeian foundation of enumeration. Once discovered by the fundamental samplings, the nice connectedness of the cosmos can aggrandize and facilitate our new inductions, but it could never have primed the inductive pump in the first place, and knowledge of the connections even now is efficacious only so far as it gives rise to statistics of classes. The abstract universal, which determines a statistical population, has the last word, and not the concrete universal, the principle of systematic completeness and coherence. There is no 'field logic' to oppose to 'class logic'. Fields may be profitable stuff for the churn of the class logic — fields and their members comprise classes — but they no more demand or permit a peculiar logic than do turnips or comets. If enumerative induction is 'puerile' it is so only in being *primary*, the indispensable boy who is father to the man of developed knowledge. Without it to ground at least the most general uniformities, Bacon's tables and Mill's methods and Galileo's and Einstein's analytic intuitions would be chaff on the wind.[3] On the other hand, whereas no finer canons of inquiry are of any use without the sampling principle, the sampling

---

[3] The special stricture of Bacon, repeated by Mill, Green, and others (see Hibben, *op. cit.*, p. 192), that an enumerative induction (with a universal conclusion) is always subject to overthrow by a single adverse instance, can only be called monstrous. Any universal generalization, however established, including the principles of the multiplication table, would be overthrown by a single adverse instance. In the case of the multiplication table we can be sure *a priori* that there is no adverse instance. With respect to the laws of nature we cannot be sure, and any inductive theory which implies that we can is simply false. Our own merely approximative or 'moral' universals are in a sense immune to overthrow by a single instance, but they can be overthrown by sufficient runs of adverse instances.

principle is valid and useful without any other principle. It is hence not the case, as Keynes and Mill have argued,[4] that sheer multiplication of instances, all alike, will add nothing to the credibility of a generalization. Variety of instances we have admitted as a subordinate criterion, but it plays no part in the fundamental probabilities yielded by our sampling formula, which are abundantly forthcoming no matter how similar the instances may be.

A result of our inductive philosophy, in short, is that 'the logic of science', so often treated as a branch of psychology, shop practice, etiquette, or pragmatic morals, *is* logic. The principles of 'problem solving', 'inductive methodology', 'scientific procedure', and 'the confirmation of hypotheses' are as formal, abstract, and necessary as any of the theorems of mathematical logic. The principles of induction and hypothesis are no less *a priori*, no more mental or operational, than the syllogism or the calculus. It is hence a fundamental error to contrast, in the first place, the principles of induction and hypothesis with those of the syllogism on the ground that the former are somehow more 'concrete' and 'material', the latter more 'abstract' and 'formal'. The inductive principles are expressible in the same systematic and schematic symbolism, with the same class variables and with cognate logical constants, and like the principles of deduction are utterly general principles concerning all propositions of certain logical forms. In the second place, then, the principles of inductive probability are no less 'hypothetical', and no more so, than the principles of deduction. Both are 'hypothetical' in two senses which we observed in Chapter 2: each conveys that *if* two propositions are of such and such forms, then *if* the one is true, the other is true (with certainty or with a stipulable probability, as the case may be). Neither kind of principle is 'hypothetical' in the sense of being itself a hypothesis or a postulate or contingent on a hypothesis. It is a fundamental error, accordingly, in the third place, to speak of inductive logic as especially an 'applied' logic, or a 'logic of truth', or a 'factual' logic, in contrast with the deductive 'logic of consistency'. In one sense, all logic is 'applied logic', in the sense, namely, that it *applies* — its sentences are descriptive of what is the case. In another sense, no logic *per se* is intrinsically 'applied'. A branch of logic consists of a body of very general principles which may or may not be recognized by us in their exemplifications, and which may or may not be utilized to infer from true premises. In some senses, again, all logic is a logic of 'truth': its own propositions are true, and many of them, at least, are *about* truths, in that they determine what follows for the truth of a consequent from an assurance of the truth of an antecedent. No logical principle, on the other hand, inductive or deductive, is otherwise concerned with the truth of the said antecedent (except as the same or a different principle may be adduced in turn to justify that antecedent as the consequent of an ante-antecedent).

If now, in the fourth place, there is still some point in calling the part of logic which embraces the principles of induction and hypothesis "empirical logic", this can only be by metonymy, because it is the logic most prominently characteristic of the procedure of so-called 'empirical science' and because it is commonly employed on premises which are especially close to the raw deliverances of sense experience. The principles neither of induction nor of deduction are empirical propositions themselves; the principles both of deduction and of induction are true equally of empirical and of non-empirical premises.

The only excuse, if there be such, fifthly and finally, for dubbing the principles of induction and hypothesis "the logic of discovery" or "the theory of inquiry" or "heuristic theory", in contrast with the deductive 'logic of proof', must reside in whatever is the sense in which induction is 'ampliative' and deduction is only 'explicative', and this sense is not easy to expound. In the respects ordinarily bruited there is no such difference. We may be said to employ a principle of inference, inductive or deductive, for 'proof' when, having both the premise and the conclusion already in mind, we observe or proclaim that the premise implies the conclusion. Any principle, deductive or inductive, may be said to be employed for 'discovery' when, having only the premise in mind, we have to think up a conclusion which not only follows from the premise but is appropriate to a particular purpose at the moment. Discovery is 'inference' *par excellence*. The thinking up is ordinarily, no doubt, of a somewhat higher creative order in the case of an inductive hypothesis than in a deduction, but in both cases it is a natural fact for the psychologist or epistemologist to explain. The mysteries of 'hunch', 'insight', 'creative imagination', and so forth, whose examination is so distracting in textbook discussions of the logic of induction, are no special prerogatives or liabilities of inductive logic. For the logician all that is relevant is that the conclusion, however apocalyptic its advent, turn out to be implied, demonstratively or probably, by the premise. Logic, either deductive or inductive, furnishes a touchstone by which a person can judge retrospectively whether he has thought validly, and he may mend his ways accordingly, but logic, deductive or inductive, does not otherwise prescribe to us 'procedures' or 'how to think'.[5]

There is nothing esoteric, then, about the authority of modern science. Science is not, or should not be, a cabal with a ritual of grips and passwords. Its prestige is not dependent, like a magician's, on the marvels it has done, nor like the pro-

[5] G. Pólya, in an interesting study, "Heuristic Reasoning and the Theory of Probability", *American Mathematical Monthly*, Vol. XLVIII, 1941, p. 464, has supposed that the 'transitory and provisional' character of the results of scientific confirmation proves that inductive principles are especially 'heuristic' and not properly part of 'logic' in the ordinary sense. This 'provisional' character, however, only marks the difference between probability logic and demonstrative logic. It is our familiar principle that the probability of a given conclusion will be different in relation to different evidence. It pertains no more to inductive than to deductive probabilities, and it involves 'heuristics' only in the sense that a familiar aspect of the process of discovery is an increase of evidence and hence an exchange of probabilities. At every stage the probability relation between the current premise and the conclusion is logical and eternal, no more transitory than an entailment.

priety of taking snuff, on its being the custom of a ruling caste. It is the practice of logic, accumulating the evidence which the logic of induction declares to be most decisive and collating the hypotheses for which it decides. Knowledge is scientific just so far as it does enact and apply the logic of induction and hypothesis; the method of science consists of the active expedients which are dictated by this aim. Controlled observation, measurement, and experiment, so reverently acclaimed in some popular studies of the subject and so roundly contemned in others, are not the heart and arcanum of science but they are among the best of those expedients. There is no intrinsic virtue, for example, in pointer-readings or in the instigation of evidence by manual experiment. It only happens that some of the kinds of evidence which inductive logic decrees to be especially decisive are ordinarily unobtainable without such instigation. If the same or equally relevant evidence should occur without our lifting a finger — and it sometimes does — it would have the same logical effect and be so much the cheaper, cleaner, and more convenient. Even the fact that scientific conclusions 'work', providing us the means of better living, confirms them only so far as the working is one of the consequents predictable from the hypotheses, and then only the truth of the prediction and not its usefulness is what does the confirming. A planned and predicted string of catastrophes would do as well.

If there is doubt of the propriety of the phrase "logic of science" it pertains to the adequacy of "science" and not of "logic". In its ordinary acceptation "science" stands for just a few isolated professional disciplines. These, to be sure, are notable for their especially clear-cut, deliberate, and elaborate use of inductive principles, but the methods of science based on those principles are reasonableness and right-headedness in action, and are operative therefore in all intelligent living. There is just one scientific logic and one fundamental scheme of method for all the sciences, whether of nature or of society, whether of fact or of value, but the same logic and method must prevail also in valid conclusions and prudent behavior of every

day, in keeping house, in marrying, in doing a job, in diagnosing
a disease, in voting a ticket, in convicting a criminal. While we
exalt scientific inference we must not forget that the ordinary
man, and the scientist in his ordinary capacity, make more confirmations and inductions in a day than a practicing college of
scientists is likely to. Since life and death, happiness and
misery, are more often at stake in those diurnal inferences —
the results of marrying the wrong woman may be more per-
manent and disastrous than the results of ascribing the wrong
molecular structure to a new protein — they may be made more
seriously and responsibly than most scientific pronunciamentos.

As the services of the inductive principle are of the same
quality and urgency in science and in responsible common life,
so are they the same, in science, for the realistic and the posi-
tivistic interpretations of that activity. The logic of induction
is both necessary and sufficient to explore what S. C. Pepper
calls the 'middle-sized facts' of daily life, or strings of sensations,
or ontologically independent things in themselves. The operationalist and positivist will interpret scientific statements as
concerned with the first or the second of these categories, the
realist with the third, but all must use the same logic, and trust
its validity to the same principles, to infer from the present data
to their respective ulterior objects, none of which is totally
present *now*. In many instances the realist, at any rate, may
employ the one set of sampling observations in either of two
ways, as symptomatic of the composition either of an antecedent class of independent objects or of an extended sequence
of further observations. Thus if I have inspected a hundred
beans from a bag and found about three-fourths of them black,
I can infer inductively either that about three-fourths of the
beans in the bag are black or that about three-fourths of my
selections from the bag will be black. The inspected beans, in
other words, constitute at the same time a sample of the beans
and a sample of my inspections. The logic of their latter rôle
is a little simplified if the beans are taken out and replaced one
by one, in which case the inspection population may be much

greater than the bean population, though in all likelihood its composition will be the same. In inferring that the next bean selection will be black, then, I can treat it by reference to either the bean population or the inspection population. We have in these chapters always preferred the former interpretation; the positivist and operationalist again will prefer the latter.

Since the sampling principle is logically necessary and absolutely universal, it can be applied to inductive principles themselves, and it is an odd and somewhat confusing fact that many of the detailed and ramified inductive canons which we sketched earlier in this chapter were actually worked out by simple inductive experiment. Most scientists and many suggestible philosophers of science are loath to admit that their canons of confirmation exemplify the stark necessities of an abstract and analytic logic just because they have themselves so recently come upon them the hard way, by inductive cut and try. Conversely, just because their inductive trials were valid and generally successful, their fallacious epistemology has done less harm to their practice, and a more formal inductive logic may now do less good, than might have been expected.

We warned ourselves earlier against the error of supposing, because the natural laws discovered by the sciences are concatenated in mutual support, that they must be intrinsically necessary, not requiring sampling to disclose them. We can take heed now of an opposite error, sometimes exemplified by the same persons, of supposing, because the principles of induction and hypothesis are, naturally enough, habitually successful, that they are themselves mere empirical generalizations, with no warrant except successful sampling. If the sampling principle itself had no warrant but sampling, it would of course have no warrant at all. If we admit that all true propositions, taken one at a time, can be inductively confirmed, we still cannot admit that all knowledge can rest on inductive confirmation alone. Induction is valid, including the induction of inductive principles, because the ultimate inductive principle is also a logical necessity in its own right.

Since scientific logic is logic, *a priori* and analytic, there is little likelihood that its principles can be very adequately investigated by an anthropological study of science as a folkway, in the manner advocated by idealists, pragmatists, and positivists. They are rather to be understood and revised by logical analysis and deduction. Correspondingly it is not likely that inductive principles now current among the more sagacious scientists and jurists, for example, will succumb, like mere empirical hypotheses, as pragmatic methodologists predict, to quite other and even incompatible maxims to emerge in the course of the adjustment of human inquiry to its environment. The metamorphoses to be expected in inductive logic are of a rather slower and slighter sort. It is possible to make a mistake even about analytic truisms, including the canons of induction and hypothesis, but changes in the logical sciences have come about much less by the rectification of such errors, to say nothing of revolutionary reconstruction, than by a progressive refinement, enlargement, and systematization. The current principles of induction and hypothesis will undoubtedly be enlarged and refined upon, and it is possible that some newly deduced principles will dwarf or displace the present favorites as instruments of research. It is hardly conceivable that the current principles will be denied, however, nor even that the law of simple sampling and some of the primary lessons of Bayes' theorem will cease to carry the main burden of the inductive venture, any more than the multiplication table or the *modus ponens* has been superseded by any of the niceties of modern mathematical logic.

6

THAT INDUCTION PRESUPPOSES NOTHING

It is not to be expected that a philosophical analysis, like our account of induction, even though it is mainly compiled of ideas which are common property among those interested in the enterprise, will make its way at the first hearing. The human mind, and notably the philosophic mind, needs more than proof, prosaically assembled of true premises and valid inferences. It needs also persuasion, a rhetorical kneading of the brain surfaces, until the ruffled spirit is reconciled and the idea is absorbed and habituated. In the present slim volume I do not have the scope even if I had the talent for such conciliatory massage. There are a recurrent few sorts of resistance to our project, however, less mute and stubborn, which suggest respects in which our study is obscure or unprepossessing and which call for correction and reply. Although we run a certain danger in refuting refutations which most readers would not think of for themselves, there is compensation in the better perspective in which the topic is thereafter understood.

The doubts which we have to drag into the open and defeat are such as go straight to the heart of our philosophy, the thesis that the inductive principle is part of logic. Objections to the idea of logical connection in general, demonstrative or probable, and to the idea of probability logic in particular, we treated as carefully as we can now afford in Chapters 2 and 3. The fact that those objections are raised with redoubled fury when the hypercritical mind sees the significance added to logic and probability by our derivation of the inductive principle is a tribute to the persuasiveness of the latter. We have now to contemplate only the doubt or denial that, granted the general validity and pertinence of logic and probability, it is conceivable that there should be an *a priori*, presuppositionless logic of induction. Since we have just witnessed a better than middling proof that there is an inductive logic, and what it is, some of us may boggle a little at diffuse and merely dialectical arguments that an inductive logic cannot exist — arguments awkwardly reminiscent of the attempt of Galileo's Peripatetic rivals to conjure Jupiter's moons out of the sky with Aristotelian texts. Not to evade an issue, however, let us review the arguments in their two main sorts: contentions that logic and induction are in essence and principle such that the one cannot vindicate the other, and contentions that our effort to vindicate induction depends in fact upon certain specifiable presuppositions or assumptions outside of logic.

Among the first contentions belongs a somewhat indefinite charge that our venture would 'turn induction into deduction'. The easy reply to this would be that in so far as we do prove that induction is a species of the genus deduction, a good philosopher, however little he might have expected it beforehand, ought to accept the result with natural piety. The more attentive reply, however, is that we have actually made out distinctly just what is the difference between induction and deduction. We have found that they are both logical procedures. We have found, too, that they are linked by the fact that the cardinal inductive principle is derivable by a very special non-empirical variety of statistical syllogism, usually reckoned as a source of 'deductive probability'. Beyond this minimum rapport, however, we have left the distinction between induction and deduction as deep and remarkable as philosophers and logicians have generally surmised it to be.

Doubters not won by this explanation will be mostly such as

adhere to some whole negative philosophy of induction, especially the philosophy of Hume and the neo-positivists which
alleges that the problem of induction is a 'pseudo-problem'.
Naturally, again, if we have given a valid solution of the problem
we know that it is not a pseudo-problem. The allegation, however, is just an indomitable way of denying that induction does
have a logical basis, including the basis we attribute to it, plus
a declaration of intent to accept the results of induction regard-
less. Practically, we long since pointed out, this striking combination of skepticism and credulity may be more dangerous
than the purer, paralytic variety of skepticism. Theoretically,
until it has impugned our solution in detail, it has no better
recourse against us than appeal to the authority of David Hume
and of a related epistemological theory, currently popular, that
logical implication can be only explicative and never ampliative.

Though we have managed to make only glancing reference
to Hume, we know that he has been for two hundred years the
great adversary of inductive validity, and it is so widely supposed that 'Hume has been master, only to be refuted in the
manner of Diogenes or Dr. Johnson',[1] that a frequent blanket
indictment of our essay will be that it cannot be right because if
it were right Hume must have been wrong. Since there is excellent indication that Hume knew and cared remarkably little
about the logic of statistics and probability, this elevation of him
to premier authority might have dumbfounded even *le bon David*
himself. Hume has an incontrovertible claim on our gratitude
for rounding off an intellectual period, for installing the elements of the inductive problem as a familiar part of our heritage,
and for making more thorny the path of obscurantists coming
to pull the wool over our eyes. The credulous skepticism which
he reached, however — the doctrine of animal faith so decisively
opposed to ours — was reached not by refuting our thesis or
any of our arguments for it, but by stubbornly ignoring its
possibility. In spite of the better example of Joseph Butler, the
mathematicians, and the gamesters, he assumed without debate

[1] J. M. Keynes, *A Treatise on Probability*, p. 273.

that there could not be a logic of probability and hence that if there is no apodeictic justification of induction there is no logical justification of it at all.

If we neglect Hume's positivism, his occasional opinion that the world exists only as a fabric of experience, and his rare doubts concerning the validity even of demonstrative 'reason', neither of which had anything special to do with his more memorable theses, his crucial contentions with respect to induction were three. (1) There is not a necessary or intrinsic implication between the inductive subject M and the inductive predicate P, and hence the truth of *All M is P* cannot be apprehended by rational intuition, or by the law of non-contradiction, as can that of $2 + 2 = 4$ or *All parrots are birds*. (2) There is not a necessary or intrinsic implication between the inductive premise, *All MQ is P*, and the inductive conclusion, *All M is P*, and hence the latter cannot be strictly deduced from the former. (3) There is a psychological propensity, however, when we have observed that all *MQ* is *P*, to expect all *M* to be *P*.

None of these propositions, true or false, it will be observed, affects our validation of induction. I believe in fact that they are generally true, and for good measure we have been taking them for granted. Hume could suppose himself to have precluded thereby a logical justification of induction only because, giving the name "probability" to the mere psychological propensity, as it is exhibited in different degrees in different sampling situations, he arbitrarily omitted consideration of a non-demonstrative logical implication either between the subject and the predicate or between the premise and the conclusion of the inductive inference. Certainly the psychological fact that when we have observed that all *MQ*s are *P* we are inclined to expect all *M*s to be *P* is no more an indication that there is not also a logical implication between them than our even more decided propensity, when we have accepted the premises of a mathematical demonstration, to accept its conclusion, is a disproof of its logical validity. On the contrary, we should expect that in a biological species fit for survival the propensity to believe would be positively rather than negatively correlated with real logical cogency.

There is in Hume just one argument, though several times repeated, which may be said actually to conflict with our inductive principle by entailing that where intuition or demonstration is futile, sampling must be futile too. It is almost his only venture into logic, and it is undefended and indefensible: that 'constant conjunction . . . can never be an object of reasoning, and can never operate upon the mind, but by means of custom',[2] so that logically we cannot 'draw from a thousand instances, an inference which we are not able to draw from one instance'.[3] That this is *ad hoc* and undefended, the reader may satisfy himself by searching the texts. That it is indefensible is attested not only by our own inductive logic now, but by its plain contradiction of even the oldest deductive logic. The proposition that my child has swallowed a thousand cherry stones is different from the proposition that he has swallowed one, and both its logical and its physiological consequents are different. *There are 1000 MQP* (a sound sampling premise) unquestionably differs therefore in many of its logical implicates from *There is 1 MQP;* and there is nothing odd in the discovery that among the differences is the fact that an induction based on the first proposition is highly probable while one based on the second is very improbable. Our argument in this book, by showing why this is the case, is an answer, too late to gratify Hume, to his honorable challenge, "I cannot find, I cannot imagine any such reasoning. But I keep my mind still open to instruction, if any one will vouchsafe to bestow it on me".[4]

[2] *A Treatise of Human Nature*, ed. Selby-Bigge (Oxford, 1928), p. 170.

[3] *An Enquiry Concerning Human Understanding*, ed. Selby-Bigge (Oxford, 1927), p. 43. The *Enquiry* contains similar passages on pp. 75, 78–79, 162, and the *Treatise* on pp. 155–156, 165.

[4] *Enquiry*, p. 36. Compare p. 34: "If you insist that the [inductive] inference is made by a chain of reasoning, I desire you to produce that reasoning. . . . There is required a medium, which may enable the mind to draw such an inference, if indeed it be drawn by reasoning and argument. What that medium is, I must confess, passes my comprehension; and it is

In the neo-Humean skepticism of today, perhaps less hospitable to instruction than the great original, Hume's dictum that whatever is distinguishable is separable, the root of his denial of necessary connection between cause and effect and between sample and population, is coupled with an extreme variety of the theory that logic is purely analytic or 'tautologous', to wit, that 'if p follows from q, the sense of "p" is contained in that of "q"',[5] so that 'in no way can an inference be made from the existence of one state of affairs to the existence of another entirely different from it'[6] So far as affects the admittedly explicative inferences of deduction this is not especially ominous. Most of us are reconciled more or less to the reflection that a logically valid deduction cannot rise higher than its source nor produce something which was not somehow implicit in the premise. To the supposedly ampliative inferences of induction and hypothesis, however, it would appear to be fatal.

Now the one really correct reply to this kind of stricture, we must insist again, is that if our critics' philosophy of logic entails that induction cannot be valid, the validity of induction equally entails that their philosophy of logic is false; and that we have here made out a better case for the validity of induction than they ever have for their philosophy of logic. It will be politic, however, to observe just wherein the conflict lies and how much is avoidable.

---

incumbent on those to produce it, who assert that it really exists, and is the origin of all our conclusions concerning matter of fact". There could hardly be a nicer statement of the issue which this monograph is designed to meet. If we suspect its good faith, we do so because we surmise that Hume intended to demand that we prove it demonstratively impossible for an inductive premise to be true and its conclusion false, a demand which is self-evidently absurd both logically and empirically.

[5] L. Wittgenstein, *Tractatus Logico-Philosophicus* (New York and London, 1922), p. 107. The quotation marks within the quotation are Wittgenstein's. By a "p" in quotation marks he apparently intends, not to name the letter "p", as we do, but to express something like what is meant by the descriptive phrase "the sentence which expresses the proposition p".

[6] The same, p. 109. "Entirely different" (German "gänzlich verschieden", p. 108) apparently means just *numerically distinct*.

Some concession to a crude logical conservation principle, *Nothing comes from nothing*, is contained in our admission that when we pass from explicative to ampliative inference we must relinquish demonstration-cogency for mere probability-cogency. There is no simple proportionality, however, between the degree to which an induction is ampliative and the degree to which it is probable, and the concession will in any case hardly placate a critic who objects that there can be *no* logical connection between distinct facts.[7] He may put his point in this way: *The sun will rise tomorrow* is certainly not strictly deducible from, because it is nohow 'contained in', *The sun has risen every twenty-four hours in the past.* If now we pare our conclusion to *Probably the sun will rise tomorrow*, there are two possibilities. The new conclusion may be genuinely contained in the premise, and then it is not really about tomorrow but is only a peculiar way of excerpting or digesting something about past sunrises. On the other hand, the conclusion may really be about tomorrow, and then it altogether transcends its premise, is independent of it, and cannot validly be inferred from it.

This argument, we already know, cannot be correct as it stands because a probability conclusion is not of the form of *It is probable that the sun will rise*, related by a demonstrative implication to its premise; it is of the form of *The sun will rise*, related by a probability implication to its premise. (See page 46.) Just how a probability implication does compare with a demonstrative implication and whether its consequents can transcend their antecedents at all, or can do so in a sense in which those of a demonstrative implication cannot, is a question to be settled not by surrender to some semantic theory but by painstaking examination of what in fact they do, and this is just what we have been attempting. In the simple proportional syllogism, as also in the Aristotelian syllogism, it seems appro-

---

[7] "No logical implication" would be more accurate. That Mars has twice as many moons as the Earth constitutes a 'logical connection' of some sort between a fact about Mars and a fact about the Earth. Hume's usage would frequently benefit from this kind of emendation.

priate to say that the conclusion does not transcend its premises. In induction, it seems more appropriate to say that it does. That this seems appropriate in the case of induction is due to the use in the latter of that surprising principle — rule of inference or *a priori* premise as you like — the logical law of large numbers.

However little the unbeliever might have expected it, it is a necessary truth, certifiable by conceptual analysis and demonstration, that if M is a class, and MQ a subclass, and P is any predicate, then if $[MQ]$ is large, MQ is one of a class of subclasses of M, all of the same size $[MQ]$, among which the great majority are statistically similar to M with respect to P, and that consequently an inference that the composition of the population M is similar to the composition of the given sample MQ is one of a great number of possible inferences, with true premises, in which the great majority have true conclusions. In just this way, then, in the teeth of all misgivings, there does exist among the members of any population, and hence among all sets of objects in the universe, past, present, or future, a logical connection which permits at least probable inference from some to others. The hydrogen atoms of the earth's surface are bound together with the hydrogen atoms in the farthest star in the nebula in Andromeda in a logical lattice by which the nature of the one is validly symptomatic of the nature of the other. We can suit ourselves whether we say now that since the connection is necessary it is after all 'merely analytic', or that since it is a connection of distinct facts it must be 'synthetic'. I incline without ardor to the former. It has never been at all clear in what sense even a deductive conclusion is 'contained in' its premise, except that it just is deducible from it, so we need not wonder that it is unclear whether and how an inductive conclusion is contained in its premise.

The logical connection on which we found induction is not intensional, holding between properties as such (universals or essences or predicates), but extensional, holding between classes or sets. We have asserted no logical implication between a thing's being a crow and its being black, nor between some crows' being black and other crows' being black. The crowness and blackness enter our accounting only accidentally and *ex post facto:* we are interested in them, but the logical law of large numbers concerns directly only the statistical interlocking of any groups or classes, as sets of individuals, irrespective of the properties by which we may find it profitable to identify them. The classes which we symbolize by "M" and "P" might be delimited by mere counting off — John Jones, the island of Malta, Sirius, the comma at the end of this phrase, and so forth — with no allusion to a common and peculiar property, and if the classes were sufficiently large our laws would still hold among them.

The remaining objections to our thesis are not whole logical philosophies, asserting that logic is too empty to justify induction, but are somewhat better documented charges that our use of the law of large numbers to defend induction depends at certain specifiable junctures on extra-logical assumptions or presuppositions about the nature of the world. If these charges were true, and induction were logically credible only in a certain kind of world, our theory would still have a sort of curiosity value, naturalizing and harmonizing the principles of induction in the current world view, but it would fail altogether of its logical purpose, since an inductive principle which depends upon a world view which can be substantiated only by induction is a principle which has no logical validity. To meet the objections once and for all, it might suffice, again, to refer to our fundamental argument and re-assure ourselves at first hand that we in fact established the validity of induction without using any ideas or propositions except those of logic — that we indulged in no whit of material assumption — but it will be expedient again to attend to the particular 'presuppositions' or 'assumptions' which, I have discovered, are most likely to be seriously imputed to us, and to show for each one either that the justification of induction does not require it or that it is not an assumption but an analytic truism.

.The most obstinate complaint, I think, among honest in-

quirers ready to admit the rest of our analysis, and with no
interest in traducing logic otherwise, is that our whole scheme
of sampling probabilities is ample and valid only on the condition that we know that the given sample is 'fair', 'unbiased', or
'random', and this knowledge our theory does not provide for.
The objection, to be sure, is at bottom identical with an objection to the major principle of statistical probabilities which we
have already considered and answered in Chapter 3. The person who demurs that the fact that most of the protosamples in a
population match the population does not make it highly probable that a given sample is one which matches unless there is some
assurance that the sample is fairly selected, is arguing in
essence no differently from the person (answered in Chapter 2)
who demurs that the fact that most of the marbles in a bag are
black does not make it highly probable that a selected marble
will be black unless there is some assurance that it is fairly
selected. Because of some peculiarities of the inductive syllogism, however, including differences between a hyperpopulation
and an ordinary population, and the signal degree of material
ignorance concerning the population and the hyperpopulation in
the normal inductive situation, the demand for fairness is
somewhat more plausible and more frequent with respect to induction, and it deserves a little special attention to make clear
that it is no less mistaken.

One interpretation of "fairness", encouraged by the fact that
the units of the inductive syllogism are subclasses instead of
ordinary individuals, we must discard at once as plainly useless:
that a 'fair' sample is a 'representative' one. If to be 'representative' of a population is merely to be a selection from it,
every sample is 'representative', while if it is to be statistically
similar to the population, and that is how we would use the word,
the demand that the sample be 'representative' is a demand that
the induction be certified as infallible in advance.

There are left now just two ways of understanding the idea of
'fairness', analogous to two which we distinguished on page
67. The first is correct but empty and redundant: our use

of the sampling law is 'fair' only if we do not know any facts relevant to our conclusion except the size and composition of the sample (which are all that the sampling law can take account of). The other is absurd and contradictory of the very concept of probability: that the use of the sampling formula is 'fair' only if we know that there *are* no facts relevant to our conclusion except the size and composition of the sample.

The demand that when we allot an inductive probability by the sampling formula we have no evidence except what the sample itself affords is our familiar truistic consequent of the truism that probability is a relation to a body of evidence, and that the probability relation of a proposition to one body of evidence (say the number and composition of the sample) is normally different from its probability relation to another. This one significant and correct demand for fairness then is merely the demand that we ignore no evidence and do not announce as the probability of our induction in relation to all the evidence what is actually its probability only in relation to part of the evidence. Here is no dead end. If the sample is not known to be unfair, that is, to be only part of the present evidence, it is fair. If it is known to be unfair, then there is other evidence which, taken together with the sample, yields a different but 'fair' probability in accordance with one or another of our probability principles. For most of us, a presidential straw vote among telephone subscribers is an unfair sampling because we know (by previous inductions, say) that having a telephone is statistically associated with an economic position associated, in turn, with characteristic political preferences. We do not despair, however. We may state a new probability, less than the pure sampling figure, that the population nevertheless matches the sample. Or we may state a greater probability that the population differs from the sample in a definable way. Or we may reject the sample and collect a new one which does not have its kind of idiosyncrasy, or which has an idiosyncrasy inductively known to be especially conducive to matching. Or we may keep the sample but consider a different population, a subpopulation, characterized by the same idiosyncrasy as the sample: a set of telephone subscribers may be a poor clue to the political opinions of Americans at large but for that very reason a good clue to the opinions of American telephone subscribers. Considerations like these are the commonplaces of inquiry. By means of them we quickly learn to trim down our inductive ambitions to comparatively narrow populations, instead of aiming at the composition of the universe. By means of them we conduct that vast complex of consilient operations which, we saw in Chapter 5, continually revise, multiply, or diminish the probative force of inductive samples.

Very different from the demand that we take account of all the relevant facts we know — and indeed that we know all the relevant facts we can — is the demand that we know that there are no other relevant facts than the ones we have, i.e., know that no further information would change 'the' probability of the proposition in question. The latter looks like only a scrupulous extrapolation from the previous rules, but it is logically nonsensical. Except when the evidence already given makes it certain, or contracertain, that the sample matches the population — and then there is no question of probability at all — the innumerable further facts about the sample must yield innumerable different probabilities, including either certainty or contracertainty, and so preclude probability again altogether.

The specific form in which the fallacious requirement is ordinarily expressed is instructive: that the population be known 'homogeneous' or 'unstratified' with respect to the moot predicate *P*. The only clear meaning which can be given to this is that we must know that in each of the different kinds or classes of protosamples included in the population there is the same proportion of population-matching groups as in the total hyperpopulation. Not only, however, would any such elaborate statistical complexion be hopelessly unknowable — incomparably more difficult to know, of course, than the composition of the population which the main inquiry is about. Like the similar demand in the simpler instance of page 68, it is logically impossible. Except when the population composition is 0 or 1, the population must contain countless subclasses of protosamples exemplifying all degrees of predominance of all degrees of approximation to the population composition. No less absurd, furthermore, are the results of qualifying our demand on the population so that we require, not that the proportion of matches be known to be the same in all the different subclasses of protosamples, but that it be known to be the same in all the subclasses of which the actual sample is a member — i.e., in the common phrase, that the sample be known to 'differ in no relevant respect' from the rest of the population.[8] Although it would be impossible again to know any fact of such prodigious scope about any sample, we can know again *a priori* that, unless the population composition is 0 or 1, any such condition is logically impossible. Every sample must belong to countless classes of protosamples evincing different proportions of matching samples, including either the proportion 0 or the proportion 1. The knowledge of these inevitable divagations causes no vertigo or disillusion to the right inductive philosopher because they are intrinsic to the logical concept of probability and are no more than the sample formula takes account of, at the most exorbitant evaluation, to begin with. Every statistical population contains not only many protosamples which don't match it but many classes of protosamples in which there are disproportionately few matches. This does not feaze our proof that it contains many more protosamples which do match, and many more classes of protosamples in which there are many matches. Until we have concrete evidence that our actual sample is a member of a specifiable class of samples which is specifiably peculiar with respect to its proportion of matches, all this abstract reflection is in the strictest sense irrelevant to the verdict of the sampling formula.

[8] A simpler and bolder interpretation of the demand that 'the sample differ in no relevant respect from the population' is that the sample, without more ado, simply *match* the population, for to say that a property R is 'relevant' to P in M is just to say that the ratio of $[RMP]$ to $[RM]$ is different from the ratio of $[MP]$ to $[M]$.

The researcher who is still uneasy at our license to trust the sampling law with no better warrant than that we do not know any other facts which are relevant, but who perceives the absurdity of demanding that we know that there are *not* any other facts which are ('would be') relevant, finds a certain release in the intermediate demand that we know at least that one rather special kind of fact is not relevant, namely, the 'method of selection'. Such seems to be the import of the demand that the sample be chosen by 'a random method'. By Jeffreys' definition this means that the sample 'is drawn in such a way that any set of that number in the population is equally likely to be taken'.[9] We saw in Chapter 2 some senses in which this kind of provision is respectively otiose, impossible, and irrelevant. Its strongest interpretation is Peirce's rule that 'the sample must be taken according to a precept or method which, being applied over and over again indefinitely, would in the long run result in the drawing of any one set of instances as often as any other set of the same number'.[10] This is still inadequate to Peirce's intention as it stands, but he clearly means a method, like that of a lottery, whose results may be presumed to have the characteristics of a statistical collective, an endless series, 'random' in the sense of being free from after-effects, in which the proportion of successes (matchings) converges toward a ratio equal to the proportion of matches in the hyperpopulation. But of what use is this requirement? Any such endless series of selections is a pure invention which belies the whole notion of sampling (whose value is predicated upon the human necessity of grabbing and running). If it were real, we should find its composition far harder to know than the composition of the original population. But if it were real, and known, it still would get us no forrader, because we should only be locating our present sampling in another reference class than our original hyperpopulation, and a reference class concerning which we know only what we already know about the original hyperpopu-

[9] Harold Jeffreys, *Theory of Probability* (Oxford, 1939), p. 48.
[10] Peirce, *Collected Papers*, II, p. 454. Cf. pp. 436, 455, 458.

lation, namely, that most of its members match the population but that lots of them do not. The new probability is the same in *quantity*, because the compositions of the original hyperpopulation and of the new selection series are by hypothesis the same. It is the same in *quality*, so to speak, with the same canker at its heart, because the selection series must have exactly as much heterogeneity as the original population: some sets of selections must be unusually good, some unusually bad, and our present actual selection may belong to a bad set. The only patent difference between the random series and the original hyperpopulation in this respect is that in the random series we are by hypothesis forever prevented from finding out *which* sets are good and which are bad, a singularly poor recommendation, one would think.

The source and excuse of so much paralyzing delicacy about probabilities is partly to be found, I think, in the human difficulty in adjusting degrees of belief to intermediate credibilities. We have little trouble with a demonstrative connection because then the evidence, however much or little we attend to it, is all one way. Probability evidence, however, always offers countervailing considerations, and if we distribute our attention unequally to the pro and the con our belief-feelings will be illogical. Now, it is notorious that, especially when we stop to think about it, we over-attend to small chances, and over-judge the resultant probability. Told in an unfamiliar context that our lives depended on a lottery with 500,000 favorable chances and 1 lethal one, most of us would be disproportionately worried, though we face worse dangers every time we motor to the beach. So too when the conscientious spirit contemplates the theory of induction, he is altogether too poignantly aware of the ways in which he may go wrong, and does not strike an equitable balance between these and the much more numerous ways in which he can go right. In particular, it is disproportionately easy to imagine gross and obvious ways of going wrong (for example, by taking our handful of beans from the top of the bag when in fact all the white ones are in the bottom) and hard to imagine gross and obvious ways of going right (for example, because the beans have been packed by a machine in a mosaic of noughts and crosses). In a particular sampling it might indeed be the case that all the white beans were in the bottom, so that in scooping from the top we were doomed to get a very poor match. It might be, however, that they were in a mosaic which made almost certain that any adjacent handful would match. And it might also be that if we had managed to number every bean in the bag and then selected a thousand 'at random' by means of a lottery or a set of Tippett's numbers, we should nevertheless have followed just the path destined to grotesque error. We have a greater horror, ahead of time, at the possibility of the first sort of aberration only because it is easily imaginable and understandable, while Tippett's numbers move in mysterious ways their blunders to perform.

The principal source, however, of the confusion which we have been examining is nothing more culpable than a conscientious garbling of the perfectly proper maxims of inductive method, that we should get all the relevant evidence we can and that we should reckon our probabilities on all the evidence we have. Civilized man has by now an enormous backlog of knowledge which alters the incidence of almost every bit of sampling. In almost every sample we recognize some oddity — like that of telephone-owning citizens — which makes it more or less likely to be a matching one than the formula alone provides, or which at any rate suggests that new evidence to that effect is so easily to be had that it is a waste of time to reckon the present probability without it. Even when we don't know specifically how the visible peculiarities of the sample are associated with the predicate *P*, we may know that they are associated with it somehow — that they are a kind of peculiarity which is generally associated with predicates of that general sort. Even when no striking peculiarities are visible, we may have good reason to conjecture that it has some peculiarities which are momentous. The uniformity of nature, the fact of stratification and real kinds, which has been widely supposed to make induction easy, and which does in some circumstances increase the probability of the universal generalizations which make induction important and useful, is actually what often makes induction hard, because it means that the conspicuous properties of the world *make a difference* to each other in such wise that strongly marked or easily netted samples are inordinately likely to be non-representative with respect to the incidence of any important predicate P. For most of our daily affairs, when we are *applying* the products of induction, we have been drilled to attend to strongly marked groups, real kinds, and we are deliberately blind to classes determined by generally irrelevant properties. Only by a difficult and artificial reversal of our natural habit can we pick out the colorless and haphazard sort of set not especially likely to be a poor sample. No wonder, therefore, that we resort in desperation to mechanisms like lotteries, whose inscrutability at one stroke relieves us of immense responsibilities and vastly simplifies our estimation, returning us to the relatively paradisal condition of 'chance'. First and last, however, in all of this, the principles of favorable cases and of pure induction remain fundamental. All the knowledge by which we correct our sampling probabilities is derived from inductions which rest ultimately on pure sampling without extraneous correction. And even now, when we have brought to bear a thousand pieces of knowledge, our finally corrected probability is only a probability, valid in spite of the fact that there are still myriads of possible corrections, further facts which *would* modify it, and that our conclusion is in actuality just true or just false.

In mentioning possible 'stratification' or 'segregation' of the population, I have meant those words in a broad logical sense to denote any statistical association of P with any properties present in the class M. In the more literal sense, however, the words refer to the association of P with a special kind of property, namely, spatio-temporal location. The marbles in a bag are in the looser sense 'stratified' with respect to whiteness, say, when the proportion of white among the glass marbles, say, is greater than among the rest. They are 'stratified' in the more literal sense when the proportion of white among the marbles on top of the pile, say, is greater than among the rest. Now, logical philosophers are especially agitated by possible unfairness engendered by this literal kind of 'stratification'. Since we are locally concentrated organisms, there are generally available to us only samples whose members occupy in common a fairly compact and continuous region of space and time: handfuls of beans, say, whose members are contiguous not only to us but to each other. The protosamples of beans whose members are remote from us or from each other do not have an equal chance of selection. On the large scientific scale we can do little or nothing to shuffle or mix our populations, and our samplings are mostly confined to the surface of this planet during a period of a relatively few years, and it is a depressing reflection that ours may be a thoroughly unrepresentative neighborhood. Logically, however, the same reply is due to this scruple as to any worry over fairness, and we have in fact taken most of our preceding examples from this sphere. No matter how thoroughly the beans or the cosmos were mixed, there must certainly be some one system of locations, continuous or discontinuous, common and peculiar to the white beans, and countless other systems which are disproportionately white or disproportionately non-white, and no matter how the sample is selected, *its* members will possess a determinate system of locations which will be included in many of those systems. It remains demonstrably true, however, that the overwhelming majority of the systems of location are not disproportionately white or disproportionately non-white, and in the absence of evidence to the contrary, it is overwhelmingly likely that the system we have hit upon is of a conformable kind.

If there is no more reason *a priori* for worrying over the common and peculiar location of our samples than over any of the rest of the many common and peculiar properties, known and unknown, which any sample or set of samples is certain to have, there is good reason *a posteriori* for further confidence. We

THAT INDUCTION PRESUPPOSES NOTHING   149

ordinarily exaggerate the extent to which our scientific samples are narrowly localized, but in any case the evidence by and large is strongly against any great relevance of space and time: the very hallmark of a genuinely philosophical and scientific mind has usually been its refusal to take seriously spatial and temporal dispersion. There are exceptions to this rule of indifference — perhaps the further nebulae are receding more rapidly than the nearer ones, for example — but the fact that we know these exceptions on the basis of inductive evidence is proof that the possibility of exceptions is no barrier to inductive knowledge.

The dread of unfairness gets its most intense and picturesque expression in the fantasy of the anti-inductive demon. How do you know, the dissenter from our thesis always sooner or later asks, that there is not a demon, of similar kidney with Descartes's mythical deceiver, who always guides our hands and eyes to non-representative samples, or changes the populations while we are thinking about them, or otherwise brings about a chronic disparity between the inductive data and the true conclusion? The answer, in the large, of course, is that we can't be absolutely sure of it, but that the possibility does not affect our inductive probabilities because it too is one among the many fantastically improbable possibilities which the sampling formula has compounded for in advance, and one which subsequent experience has made even less probable than it was before.

Our diabolists forget, in the first place, that the demon hypothesis is itself not beyond control by the evidence. We have been making inductions for a long time, many of them concerning trains of experience which have since materialized, and the results have shown definitely that no demon or other mysterious anti-inductive force has operated in *them*. Those results, together with enormous amounts of general evidence concerning the nature of things, unite to depress whatever may be the antecedent probability that a demon is hocusing us now.

Since all the actual evidence is *against* the demon, its sole credibility must issue from its abstract possibility. *A priori*, it is just one of a virtually infinite set of hypotheses, each with its repercussions on the sampling process — some hurtful, some helpful — and at worst the possibility of a malignant demon who would confound our inductions is counterbalanced by the possibility of a good sprite who would improve them. Theologians, for good reasons or bad, depose that a benign influence on induction, like the God of Descartes and the Abbé Gratry, is much more probable than a devilish one. And whereas even an indolent and feeble-minded good angel would suffice to add the little extra fillip needed to make valid inductions 100 per cent correct, only an almost inconceivably diligent and perspicacious devil could make them go wrong as much as 25 per cent of the time. The task of the anti-inductive demon, forsooth, would be less analogous to that of Descartes's than to that of the anti-entropic demon of Clerk Maxwell, imagined to defeat mysteriously the most probable distribution of gas molecules in a vessel and to corral them 'unfairly' in one end. The task of the pro-inductive angel on the contrary is like that of a spirit who would need only to improve a little on the molecules' natural tendency to randomization in order to make the number of them in every quarter almost exactly the same as in every other.

There remains the question whether a completely deceptive demon is even a self-consistent hypothesis. A blind sampling machine, incapable of conscious choice and self-correction, could not be altogether prevented from getting representative samples, but this is only because a sample which did not match one population, M, with respect to one predicate, P, must match some others of its populations in that respect and must match even M in some respects. A living mind, however, not only takes samples but makes inferences, from each sample an inference to only one population in only one respect. It seems clear, therefore, that its conclusions might in fact always be false, and conversely that a demon, or at least a demon with powers of clairvoyance or hypnosis, might indeed be unbeatable. C. S. Peirce and C. I. Lewis, however, have argued that so long as we have an untrammeled intelligence, preserving our capacity for self-correction and utilizing our labile hierarchies of inductions about inductions, like those which we observed in Chapter 5, we should get wise to the tricks of even the astutest demon.[11]

The popularity of the demon hypothesis is the last and most ingenuous witness to the great logical credibility of induction. It is the *reductio ad absurdum* of skepticism *in extremis*, aware that only by crediting a particularly incredible legend can we excuse an incredulity toward induction. It testifies that, contrary to a very widespread belief, we do not need special assistance, from God or fate, to make reasonably sure of inductive success; we require, at most, only that we not be interfered with by the most monstrous of imaginable forces. Mad as is the idea of any demon, and still more of a demon of this bizarre proclivity, it is nevertheless the most plausible alternative to inductive success, the most plausible ground of inductive failure. The dread of inductive failure is a dread that in a lifetime of millions of careful selections of samples from hyperpopulations in which on the average only two or three members out of a thousand are non-representative, we should manage continually to get hold of the non-representative ones — that the most diligent and intelligent inquiry should *cause* failure where the blindest chance would lead nearly always to success. As among the only three practical explanations for that imagined debacle, namely, a gigantic accident, composed of miscellaneous and unrelated causes, some *ad hoc* law of nature negatively correlating the complexions of things with our inductive interests, and the demon, the last shines out as, comparatively speaking, a *vera causa*.

The question whether a demon could or does defeat our inductions, be it noticed, is not the question whether inductions are logically valid, that is, really probable. Inductions are valid and probable whether there is a demon or not. The question whether a demon or something else might consistently defeat our inductions despite their great probability is the inductive version of the question whether our probabilities must mature.

[11] Peirce, *Collected Papers*, II, pp. 473–474, and V, p. 219; C. I. Lewis, *Mind and the World-Order* (New York, 1929), p. 389.

In general, we recall from Chapter 3, our theory of probabilities, although it makes very probable that our probable beliefs, including our inductions, shall in fact be true in numbers nearly proportional to their average probabilities, does not absolutely guarantee the maturity of any probability as such. What Peirce and Lewis say in despite of the demon idea entails, to be sure, that there are special qualities of induction, in contrast with ordinary marble-drawing, which guarantee that its probabilities must mature at least to the extent that we succeed more often with valid inductions than without them, but their argument seems to me unconvincing. The only circumstances in which an inductive probability could be warranted to mature are those in which we could and did draw an actual inference for every protosample contained in the hyperpopulation,[12] an entirely useless and impractical process, far more difficult than counting over the whole population to begin with. The possibility that our inductions shall persistently fail, however, instead of invalidating induction, or impugning the principles that it is reasonable to believe highly probable propositions and that valid inductions are highly probable, is simply our old corollary of the nature of high probabilities. So long as only a prodigious coincidence or conspiracy can enable even one induction to go wrong, and only an unimaginable coincidence of coincidences, or conspiracy of conspiracies, could enable any large proportion of our inductions to go wrong, induction is logically not only our best bet but a staggeringly good bet, no more reasonably to be doubted than a mathematical demonstration.[13]

When we proceed at last from considering objections to the bare idea of a logic of induction, and from the objections to probability *per se* which cause qualms about 'fairness', to strictures more immediately apposite to our theory of induction, we find them something of an anti-climax.

[12] On page 60 we treated of the non-inductive analogue of this.

[13] This is not quite to say, of course, that an induction is reasonably no more to be doubted than a demonstration, i.e., it is not to say that an induction is apodeictic.

The special presupposition most commonly attributed to justifications of induction is an assumption about the regularity or connectedness of the world — a law of causation, a uniformity of nature, a principle of sufficient reason — and this in fact has been openly postulated by most apologists. We, however, not only have not assumed any such principles but have overtly repudiated them as nuisances. We have gone along with Hume and others in denying, or at any rate ignoring, any principle of 'real' causation — that underlying the factual concomitance of a cause (the subject of a causal law) with its effect (the predicate) there is an intrinsic connection, a logical implication, or a relation of deducibility. Just how much less than logical deducibility is generally understood by "the uniformity of nature", or by "the law of causation" when the latter is used synonymously with "uniformity", is difficult to discover, but if, like "the principle of limited independent variety" of Keynes and Broad, it means that the universe shows at any rate an inordinate penchant for 100 per cent concomitances, we have provisionally accepted it as a good inductive generalization which contributes, in turn, to the inductive probability of certain specific generalizations of the 100-per-cent variety. Its efficacy, however, we have seen to depend upon a prior and purely logical validity for the induction which establishes it, and it is generally less an aid than an impediment to representative sampling. The nearest thing to a uniformity principle which we require is the fundamental law of large numbers, that most samples match their populations, and this is an analytic law of logic.

It may be imagined, notwithstanding, that we have need of at least this much assurance, that there is *some* population outside the precincts of the sample, and that it has some determinate composition with respect to the specified predicate and hence supplies some determinate proportion of matching protosamples for the hyperpopulation. We could, of course, reply that the errand of induction is to discover what is the composition of the population if there is a population and if it has a composition.

Where one of these is lacking, there is nothing for induction to discover. A more extended answer, however, may make our whole philosophy clearer.

The first apprehension, that there may be no population beyond the sample, adds to rather than detracts from the probability of an induction, for the less the population the more probable the induction. The advantage is normally inconsiderable, but if the population does not exceed the sample at all then the sample *is* the population, $M = MQ$, and the induction is a 'perfect' one and theoretically impeccable. In more normal and interesting cases, however, we have other reasons for believing that there is a large further population. Some of this further population we may simply perceive — for, as we know, we can perceive that an object is M (i.e., belongs to the population) without perceiving whether it is also P (and thus including it in the sample). More often we infer inductively, directly or indirectly, by the process described on pages 111–12, that there are more Ms. This method is as valid for temporal succession as it is for removal spacewise, and can justify at need the primal confidence, embraced in all prediction, that there will be a future. Most of us are content to know that if another twenty-four hours elapse, the sun probably will rise again, but we can also induce that another twenty-four hours *will* pass. All past moments have been followed by twenty-four-hour stretches, and many of them; it is rationally credible, to a degree so high that no ordinary wit can distinguish it from certitude, that the present moment will be so followed.

Granted that there is an ulterior population, now, it is no inductive hypothesis, and certainly no blind postulate, but a sheer mathematical necessity, that if the population is finite it must have a determinate composition. This follows from the logical laws of excluded middle and non-contradiction: everything either is a member or not a member of any stipulated class M, and nothing is both; and every member of M either is a member or not a member of MP, and none is both. There must then be determinate numbers of M and of MP, and a deter-

minate ratio, lying within the interval 0 to 1, of the second
number to the first. To defend the law of excluded middle would
be to defend logic all over again, but we can notice some of the
ideas which prompt sophistic disrespect for it in connection with
certain prominent kinds of inductive populations. Most populations, for example, would in common language be said not to be
fixed but to 'change'. From moment to moment, or from century to century, the property M (humanity or whiteness or
what not) characterizes diverse individuals, and different numbers of individuals, and within the class M there is a similar
fluctuation with respect to the members of MP, and their number, and both series of changes can bring about a fluctuation of
the ratio of the number of MP to the number of M. This however is a loose and misleading account of the business. Either
the property M contains some temporal determination (like *the
men alive at 2:15 p.m., November 4, 1944*), or the class M takes
in all individuals of a stipulated sort (*men*, for example) at all
times and places. In either event, the logical composition of the
class is fixed and changeless. If any critic is so rash as to object
that a single class cannot contain members existing at different
dates, he is simply mistaken. Common sense and ordinary
language enable us to speak of 'the popes of Rome' although it
is impossible for even two popes to exist simultaneously, and the
logic of classes on which we have depended is austerely indifferent both to the spatial and to the temporal spread of their
membership. An inclusive objection to admitting populations
containing *future* members might stem from the teaching of
Aristotle and the pragmatists that propositions about the future
can neither be true nor be false, and of C. D. Broad, for example,
that the future (even if there is going to be a future) is anyhow
ontologically *nil* for the time being. This is a very fundamental
thesis. By renouncing that timelessness of the logical forms on
which both ancient and modern authorities agree, I think it
makes all intelligible discourse impossible. By removing the
object of any prediction, at any rate, it does not so much prove
the invalidity of the inductive principle in its most important

practical use as denounce the use.[14] The one plausible source of this notion of an indeterminate future, which otherwise seems in violent conflict with both reason and experience, is nothing more redoubtable than the idea that a proposition can be neither true nor false unless we know which it is. Since we could not know except by induction, and since the validity of induction depends on the determinateness of future fact, the theory would put us in a strait jacket. Even Hume, however, though he held it is in principle impossible for us validly to confirm a belief, now, concerning the number of future sunrises, never ventured to dispute that the facts are 'there' to be guessed at. Perhaps a little more appealing, but no different logically, is the doubt whether the future is determinate in those respects in which instead of our merely not knowing what it will be, we suppose ourselves able by our voluntary action to decide what it shall be. How are we to handle, for example, a conviction that three-fourths of our bullets *would* hit the target *if* we should fire them? This raises interesting problems in the analysis of some classes of conditional statement which we would normally express in the subjunctive mood of grammar, but I do not think it affects the logic on which we have been relying.[15]

If there is a logically respectable excuse for fearing that some

[14] Since the pragmatists in particular teach both that there is no truth about the future and that all propositions are predictive, their epistemological quandary if not inextricable is unenviable.

[15] Since most readers of philosophical essays have heard of 'the principle of indeterminacy', we cannot afford not to mention it. In the accounts understandable by the layman it is alternately expressed as the propositions that certain sub-microscopic events are *undetermined*, that is, irregular, and that they are actually *indeterminate*, that is, uncharacterized. The first of these is certainly neutral to our philosophy of induction. The second, since it is self-contradictory by ordinary logical standards, is difficult to appraise. Since neither version, however, appears to be supported by any evidence except the inability of the investigators to ascertain how the events are regulated, or characterized, as the case may be — a circumstance which is explicable by many less prodigal hypotheses than that they are not regulated or characterized at all — it would be premature to bank on the doctrine one way or another.

of our populations will not have determinate compositions, it is not the dread lest there be no population nor that the members singly will not be either P or *non-P*, but that the population as a whole may be infinite, and its hyperpopulation likewise; for an infinite number cannot in the ordinary sense be a term in a ratio of the sorts required for our doctrine. This threat, which we treated cursorily on page 43, is magnificently ignored by the usual conventions and practice of statisticians, especially in the common error-formulas, which are ostensibly predicated on ratios in infinite populations. The latter, however, we have admitted to be a handy fiction, introduced without further commitment, at a single point in the calculation, to derive the minimum possible probability for the inductive approximation. The usual device for acclimating ratios among infinities we have observed in the notion of the 'limit': if the members of M are ordered in a series, then we can say that there is a ratio $\dfrac{[MP]}{[M]}$ if, in longer and longer stretches of the series, the relative frequency of P fluctuates less and less about one fraction. This apparatus might be adjusted to the demands of our inductive theory, but there is little purpose in our paltering over the mathematics of infinity, because the question has pertinence only if in fact we commonly want to make inductions to infinite populations, and this we do not. The fondness of writers on induction for alluding to infinite populations is a deceptive exaggeration: when one mentions, for example, an infinite number of Negroes,[16] he surely means no more than that first and last there will have been an immoderately large number, so large that he has no hope of naming it. The prevalent opinion in the philosophy of physics and even of mathematics is that there are no literally infinite collections, and that "infinity" appears in mathematical expressions only as a convenient symbolic shortcut between one finite quantity and another. At any rate, it is a safe bet that no classes of concrete objects or events are infinite, and a dead certainty that we can get along without making

[16] See H. A. Larrabee, *Reliable Knowledge* (Boston, 1945), p. 457.

inferences about any which are infinite. There will be, all told, a finite number of swans, crows, or men. There are a finite number of electrons and quanta, and of aggregates of electrons or quanta, and a finite number of protosamples included in the whole class of such aggregates — an extremely large number, but still subject to the same prosy arithmetic as a baker's dozen. But even though *per impossibile* there were an infinite number of men, for example, the number of men in our galaxy in the next decillion of decillion of years certainly will be finite, and anybody who wants to assert (say) that all men are mortal within a larger sphere than that may multiply it by any magnitude he likes, and any real curiosity he may have, in contradistinction to a mere play of words, can always be satisfied without trenching on a literal infinity. If, at the other end of the scale, the supposed infinity of points on the path of a moving body, for example, discommodes our reckoning, we shall make no detectable error if we speak of cubic volumes of one decillionth of a millimeter each, whose number in any observable spread is finite, and whose number in the whole of space must be finite if space itself is finite, as seems likely.[17]

An interest in the determinateness of the population composition, however, is not the only professed reason for laying down as prerequisite to induction that the population not be too great. A second and perhaps more frequent motive is a widespread idea that the probability of an induction is proportional to the ratio between the size of the sample and the size of the population, $\frac{[MQ]}{[M]}$. Some writers have asserted flatly that it is equal to that ratio; others have asserted at any rate that it is so regulated by it that a very large population must mean a very small

[17] The new and inopportune prestige of the infinite in epistemological quarters is mostly due to a favorite fiction of pragmatism and positivism, that a physical fact, even so simple and singular a fact as *This is a black marble*, consists of an infinity of possible experiences. That it is a fiction hardly needs re-telling, but its fangs could anyhow be drawn by our method above.

probability, an indefinitely large population an indefinitely small probability, and an infinite population an infinitesimal probability. I have been able to discover no ground for any of this except a vague sense of fitness, augmented perhaps by a misunderstanding of one of Laplace's somewhat dubious 'rules of succession' which professes to prove that the probability of a universal induction, *All M is P*, — with no exception or margin of error — is equal to $\frac{[MQ] + 1}{[M] + 1}$. In fact, we have seen, although the size of the population is indeed inversely related to the probability of the induction, its effect for our approximative inductions flattens off so rapidly that unless the sample is nearly as large as the population the differences on this score among inferences to populations of a million, a quadrillion, and an infinity are greatly outweighed by a small and easy increment in the absolute number of the sample. Because the size of the population has so inconsiderable an effect, we have paid no attention to it, but have relied on the luxuriant enough minimum probabilities furnished by a formula assuming the worst possible case, a virtually infinite population.

No different answer, incidentally, is required by the complaint that whereas I have written as though our samples were sharply sequestrated, member by member, from the population, in much scientific and common-sense inquiry it is impossible to guard against observing and counting the same object twice, — the same crow, for example, or the same stone. The logical effect of mixing back each specimen before we take the next is in fact of the same sort as the effect of drawing the total sample from an infinite population, and is similarly inconsequential.

Concern lest the population be infinitely greater than the sample must be distinguished from the concern, occasionally expressed, that every inductive hypothesis is only one among an infinity of alternatives and hence starts under a hopeless handicap of improbability. The composition of a population, to be sure, may take as many values as there are members of the population (this is the connection between the present doubt

and the preceding one), and *a priori* the probability of any
exactly determinate one of them is very small, approaching the
infinitesimal as the population approaches the infinite. Our
scheme of induction, however, does not fix upon one exactly
determinate composition but only on a certain range of approximation, and, unlike some theories of inductive probability,
neither does it make any use of the conception of so-called
'prior' or *a priori* probabilities for the sundry possible population compositions. It assigns probabilities solely on the basis of
empirical data which make the number of antecedent possibilities irrelevant. *A priori*, John Jones might marry any one of
the billion women on earth, but this does not at all shake our
confidence, when we have seen the knot tied, that the one he
actually married is Sarah Smith.

There is one more respect in which doubters of induction have
sometimes thought that the alternative possibilities must be
limited before induction is valid: not just that the population be
finite within which the predicate *P* is distributed, but that *P*
itself be one of a very few alternative or contrary predicates
distributed therein. Clearly this demand has no excuse in the
terms of our inductive analysis. We need take account of only
P and *non-P* (red and not red, for example), and have no concern with how *non-P* is divided, whether it is all characterized
by the same contrary of *P* (white, for example), or is all different (blue, white, gold, etc., etc.). If the sample is variegated,
we can calculate the probable variegation of the population,
with no new apparatus, by taking the contrary properties one
at a time.

This easy consideration gives us in principle the reply to the
query whether induction would work in a population, or a universe, in which every object or event was unique in the sense
that none shared any property with any other. This supposal,
in the first place, not only is contrary to the facts of immediate
experience, which plainly exhibit a tissue of similarities and
classes, but is logically impossible. If, for instance, things differed with respect to simple or determinate characters, they

must be similar with respect to complex or less determinate characters. If one thing were crimson and one scarlet, they must both be red; if one were red and the other green, both must be either-red-or-green; if only one thing were red, all other things must be non-red. All pairs of things would be alike in that their members differed from one another. All collections of a hundred things each would be alike in being mixed or motley. Even in the most chaotic world, if we could exist at all, we should speedily infer to these and countless other common characters. If things could be and were all different, however, our inductive principle, far from being estopped, would become infallible. The worst that could happen to us inductively would be to infer, for example, from the fact that there is one crimson object in a sample of 2500 that the proportion of crimson objects in the population at large does not differ from $\frac{1}{2500}$ (i.e., .0004) by more than .01, while the proportion of non-crimson objects does not differ from .9996 by more than the same amount. And this conclusion not only would be validly probable on the evidence; it is by hypothesis true. Even the inconsiderable error introduced when we infer above that crimson occurs throughout the population with the same relative frequency as in the sample would be speedily corrected as returns mounted to prove the second-level induction that no two individuals in the population were alike. The real rub in such a preternaturally variegated universe would not be a difficulty in inferring the approximate compositions of its populations, but that the compositions, even if known exactly, would be miserably unhelpful toward predicting a single case.

Our philosophy of induction, to sum up, presupposes nothing — unless by some sad perversion of language we mean by "presuppose" simply *assert*. All that it asserts are analytic laws of logic and arithmetic, each of them perspicuously necessary and inevitable in its own right, and to assert only these is the express opposite of 'presupposing' something in the significant sense of that word. We do not, it will be observed, even presuppose that there are not other supports of induction than we have depended on. We simply have not presupposed that there are, and we have defended induction by exhibiting its cogency under the worst possible conditions in any conceivable realm of being.

There are still plenty of deficiencies in the philosophy and logic of probability and confirmation which I certainly cannot boast of supplying. I have already confessed to problems concerning the compounding of probabilities and particularly concerning the choice or cumulation of 'the' probability of a proposition from the various probabilities it may inherit from different batches of evidence. I suspect that there remains more to be said on the topic of 'fairness', and there is need for deeper and more delicate study of the fundamental subject of the maturity of the chances as it comes to a head in the question of the ultimate epistemic appeal of inductive probabilities which may not mature. There are questions too concerning what Keynes calls "weight" and the logical obligation to base our probabilities on as much evidence as possible, and also concerning the claims of divers principles of analogy and parsimony, including the analysis of logical simplicity or economy and its effect on probability. In a rather different direction there is reason to question the unequivocalness of the formula of the statistical syllogism in certain peculiar situations where it appears to derive different probabilities for the same conclusion in relation to equivalent premises. In the area of induction and hypothesis there is a question of the validity of Peirce's principle that only 'predesignated' evidence is cogent, and there are so-called 'paradoxes of confirmation', such as the problem whether and why we may not count all the instances of *non-P-non-S* as confirmatory of the generalization *All non-P is non-S*, and hence, by logical contraposition, of *All S is P*. All these, however, are growing pains of a subtle and lively subject, and may be safely left to the excellent authorities now engrossed with them. They present no special obstacle to our primary **inductive** principle.

7

INDUCTION IN PHILOSOPHY

To solve the problem of induction is to solve a major problem of philosophy, perhaps *the* major problem of analytic or critical theory of knowledge. To solve it in our terms, moreover, is to establish for induction a place in the world and in knowledge which will enable the solution or partial solution of many other philosophical problems not at first obviously related to it. In the latter capacity, our account provides at once not only a logical justification but a natural history of induction, an explanation of how perception operates and why intelligence succeeds. Its most revolutionary philosophical consequents, however, will be indirect: since it is analytic and presuppositionless, necessarily valid for any entities whatever, it establishes what many have suspected but did not prove, that the empirical method of the special sciences is in its essence competent and authoritative in all the branches of philosophy also — that inductive confirmation, assisted by conceptual analysis, and not guesswork or intuition or inspiration, is the one credible organ of knowledge with respect to even the finest or massiest topics in ontology or cosmology.

In describing the logical cogency of induction, we by the same act explain why as a mundane process it commonly works, getting along profitably and veridically enough without a special principle of metaphysical harmony, or prehension, or intentional inexistence. To explain our faculty of empirical knowing, the only assurances we require are, first, that when living creatures or minded organisms encounter and are stimulated by objects of certain sorts evincing certain characters in certain proportions, they shall be caused to expect further objects of those sorts to evince the same characters in approximately the same proportions, and second, that in point of fact the objects thus encountered generally *are* representative of their classes in the requisite way.

Now, the first requirement is met in natural fact by the ABC of biopsychology, the law of conditioning or association, which is common to animals from the amoeba to man. This is itself ascertainable by induction and is explicable in turn by wider generalizations, such as the principle of natural selection. The causal qualities of living tissue are so tuned that contact with the members of a considerable sample of a certain population *causes* us to 'believe' (implicitly or explicitly) that the rest of the population has a similar composition, at the same time that it logically *confirms* that conclusion. So far are the supernaturalists and dualists wrong who argue that a validly knowing mind must operate immaterially and non-causally, that a physical law of conditioning can provide the perfect paradigm of the logic of inductive inference. I have no wish to tie up our logical thesis with a mechanistic psychology which for the present is having hard sledding in the profession, but it is worth noting how the parallel between the logical and the physiological principles is almost disconcertingly close. Not only is it true that the larger the sample, and hence the greater the logical credibility, the greater the normal propensity to believe; the Weber-Fechner law, which appears to be roughly characteristic of habit formation as of other vital and neural phenomena, and which may be taken then to measure the rate at which the multiplication of stimuli increases psychologically the readiness to believe, tapers off by a logarithmic function like the one by which, in the law of error, an increase in the number of data increases logically, but at a lessening rate, the objective credibility of the conclusion.

The other fact to be explained, in order to account for the success of induction, is that the objects encountered by inquisitive animals usually are representative of their classes. This is the empirical law of large numbers. No particular instance of it, of course, can be explained in detail and predicted with certainty without an exhaustive knowledge of just how and why each object happens to be noticed, and this knowledge is not in fact obtainable. Our logical law of large numbers, however, explains and predicts it in the manner normally accepted as adequate in the statistical sciences of nature. Asked why a basketful of lawn clippings contains so few four-leaf clovers, for example, we should usually be content to reply that it is because there were so few four-leaf clovers in the lawn.[1] Since the animal's experience consists of many samples lifted from a world of samples in which most samples match their populations, it would be amazing if most of his samples did not match their populations too. We should expect, furthermore, that they will match with a frequency and approximation which are generally proportional to their size, and proportional also, therefore, both to the logical probability of the inferences from them and to the psychological propensity to make those inferences.

Our theory does not make inductive error impossible — indeed, very properly, it makes some inductive error almost certain. But it shows the discovery of truth to be the natural and almost inevitable thing, and persistent error the merest residuum of coincidence and accident.

In his *Wahrscheinlichkeitslehre*, Professor Reichenbach summarizes his theory of induction in the parable of a blind man lost in the hills who, locating the one passable trail by taps of his stick, follows it with no better warrant than that if he is going to get home at all it must be by this trail. As contem-

---

[1] If we find this too slight an explanation, our objection, again, is not because the reply does not explain the fact queried but because the reply itself appears to require explanation. (See p. 57n.) The logical law of large numbers, however, which is our present explanation, being analytic and necessary, cannot require further explanation in the same sense.

porary attitudes go, Reichenbach's is bold and optimistic, but it is a forlorn hope compared to our present results. For if we shadow forth in a similar parable our account of induction, our situation is instead like that of a man following a trail which, though he does not know for sure that it leads to his home, he knows infallibly to be one of a thousand trails in that locality among which nearly all do lead to his home. Even this amendment, however, does less than justice to our account, because our protagonist is not blind and need not choose one trail once and for all. He can pick his trail by following a fore-path which he knows to be one of many such paths of which the majority lead to groups of trails of which, in turn, especially large majorities lead to his home. Furthermore, the trails are such that the further he finds any one trail to proceed in a uniform direction, any direction, the surer he can be that it is one of those which go in the right direction.

Combined with what was conveyed at the end of Chapter 3, these reflections should show the way to the final answer to the accusation that confidence in induction and scientific method is mere 'faith' or 'dogma', as they should dispose also of the fear that induction is 'a guessing game in which we have so far had surprising luck',[2] to be accounted for, if at all, by some beneficent cosmic dispensation. The only dispensation which we require is logical, that the universe should not contradict itself. We leave no room, then, for the dismal premonition, revived in Spencer and Santayana from ages of more religious skepticism, that there is an Unknowable, Beyond the Veil, which our very nature as percipient animals prevents us from grasping. Whatever else Reality may be, it is certainly a population, and contains only populations, which conform to the logical law of large numbers. Most selections from it must be representative of it, and what occurs in our perceptual experience is a selection from it. This is a selection, furthermore, which was scooped by a sentient and educated and educable system of living fibers whose

[2] The phrase is Broad's, in *Mind*, Vol. XXIX, p. 11, though it does not altogether represent his own position.

progenitors for a billion years have survived and perpetuated their kind just in proportion as they have mastered the knack of especially representative scooping and which in the methodology of modern science have become critically self-conscious in the procedure by which the results of the sampling process can be brought to bear to improve the probabilities of successive other results. To suspect seriously that those refinements have only led us astray is rather less reasonable than to hope that a packet of blunted razor blades will sharpen themselves by the accidents of molecular attrition, or that a strewn carload of anagram chips will spell out the cantos of *Paradise Lost.*

The comparisons in the last sentence are startlingly instructive. Most of the processes of life and culture — digestion, the writing of a book, building a bridge — are anabolic, the erection of toppling segregations and complexities against the pull of entropy: improbable, unrandom, and unstable arrangements. Induction, however, is catabolic. In the process of induction our minds fight, for once, on the side of the biggest battalions, on the downhill slope of entropy, the automatic world tendency to randomization and equalization. Most of the complex, viable, or useful structures in which we are interested, men or machines, are much more difficult to make or repair than to damage or destroy. Because there are so many more ways of marring them than of making them, most of the vicissitudes which they can undergo will mar them. A correct induction, however, is on exactly the same principle much easier to make or to rectify than to fail in, because there are so many more ways of its going right than of its going wrong. If there is any puzzle about induction, I fear, it is how we manage to go wrong as often as we do.

Our examples of the logic of induction and the correlative explanation of the actual success of inductive intelligence may be said to take *perception* for granted — that is, they make the common-sense assumption that we can perceive the existence and nature of concrete objects in order to ground the inductive premises. The problem of induction, we said, is not the problem of justifying perception, but the problem, granted the perceptual premises, of justifying the inference to the rest of the population. It is no more incumbent on us than on other philosophers of logic to enter the epistemological disputes about perception, to ask, for example, whether perceptual judgments concerning concrete things, like chairs and birds, depend logically upon inductions from a direct cognition of sense data, like klangs and light flashes, which in turn is certain and incorrigible, or are the most primitive of judgments, prior to merely sensory apprehension, and all alike fallible and corrigible. Does memory, especially, involve a kind of hypothesis based upon a present imaginal content, or is it a direct perception of the past? It helps place our theory, however, and show its philosophical importance, to remark that far from depending on the validity of perception, it is the principle on which the validity of perception can finally be established.

There is no great enigma about perception if we confine our attention either to the side of behavioral adjustment or to the side of sensory and imaginal consciousness, while the problems attached to the correlation and connection of the two sides are no more than one would expect of so fundamental an issue. In both its outer and its inner spheres or aspects, perception consists, according to the traditional and mostly correct account, in a supplementation of direct sense experience by imagination, conception, and expectation. Behaviorally, this means that when the intelligent organism has been 'conditioned' by the concurrence of sundry qualities or components of environmental objects, a new stimulation by one quality or component causes him to adjust also to some of the other associated qualities or components — the sensible contact of the color and shape of an apple, for example, provokes a complex response-attitude appropriate to its texture, its taste, its nutritive properties, and in short to 'the apple'. (This much at least is true, irrespective of the psychological fate of the simple theory of conditioning.) Phenomenally, in the subject's own experience, the sensations of red and round call up, as a result of an experience of past couplings, the various images of succulence, and so forth, and the sundry verbal tags and *Bewusstseinslagen*, which constitute 'the apple percept'. On both sides, both the practical success and the logical validity of the process are explained and predicted by our sampling theory.

"Sensationalism" is a name sometimes given to the philosophical or psychological opinion that knowledge is derived from and constituted out of distinct sensations and their correspondent images. Our inductive scheme does not at all require sensationalism as a presupposition nor entail it as a consequent: our account is equally valid and applicable if knowledge is composed of *Gestalten*, of imageless thought, of whole-situations, of 'middle-sized facts', or of commerce between things in themselves. It supports sensationalism, however, to just this extent: it shows how knowledge, with all its resources and reach, quite well *might be* built up from subjective and discrete sensa. Since the most frequent objection to sensationalism, the contention that it 'makes knowledge impossible', is thus scotched, the general force and economy of sensationalism give it a considerable advantage until its opponents can devise some more substantial objection to it.

With respect to the ultimate relation or correlation of the conscious content with the world of physical structure, my own epistemological opinions incline to the pan-objectivism of some recent British and American realists: that our perceptive experience does not consist of metaphysically sequestered states of mind nor even of neural processes inside our heads, but is composed mainly of the actual façades of the independent real objects which interact with our bodies. The pan-objectivist should blush, however, to take advantage of the usual dialectical arguments to prove his conclusion by blackening the repute of his dualistic competitors. It simply is false, for example, that 'if knowledge started with bare subjective states of mind it could never get outside to the rest of the world' and that 'the dualism of mind and nature makes knowledge an insoluble riddle'. Twentieth-century professors of philosophy have got in the way of innocently copying such slogans from each other, but anyone who tries to carry through a detailed theory of what actually happens in knowledge — an extraordinarily rare venture — must have discovered that the real puzzle on any theory is the validation of the 'leap' or 'transcendence' by which what is directly given to perception or intuition warrants a belief concerning what is not directly given. The ratio between what is given and what is known but not given is greatest on Samuel Alexander's objectivist epistemology, and is least on a simple Lockean dualism, but the logical gulf is essentially the same for both; it must be bridged for both by a theory of induction, and it is in fact bridged for both by our theory of induction, which validly reaches from anything to anywhere. Let the case be what so many of our contemporaries — neo-realists, neo-scholastics, personalists, objective relativists, absolute idealists, organicists — consider the worst possible: that the world consists of two kinds of being, extended matter and conscious mind; that a man is a neuro-muscular organism, capable of conditioned responses, *plus* a 'mind' whose content consists of a spaceless stream of sensations and images, correlated with the body's conditioning and exhibiting the Humean laws of association (or the Aristotelian). Given our principle of induction, not merely would it not be impossible for such a metaphysically bifurcated being to know what is going on in the world, including eventually his own dual nature; it would be virtually impossible for him not to know it — that is, only the most incredible bad luck could prevent him from knowing. If this is true of a crude Lockean sensationalism — combining the supposed faults of atomism and of both psychophysical and epistemological dualisms — it must be, by the ordinary account, *a fortiori* true of man as described by organismic and monistic theories.

One fact about the external world which even the most dual and introverted being must discover is that there is such a world. The formula, also copied uncritically by philosopher from philosopher, that 'solipsism cannot be refuted', is not quite false — it is true in the sense that because both solipsism and its denial transcend what is immediately perceived, it cannot be demonstratively refuted, any more than there can be demonstratively refuted that the moon is made of green cheese. The formula is almost wholly false, however, because solipsism can be refuted in the ordinary sense, the important sense, the sense in which the cheese theory can be refuted, namely, by the adduction of evidence which condemns it as a wantonly improbable hypothesis. The principles involved in the inductive proof that there is an external world are the same as are concerned in perceptual and common-sense and scientific conclusions concerning what is going on in the external world — the other side of the moon, or the other side of the earth, or the other side of the parlor door. These include plain sampling and Bayes' theorem, but especially the principles of relational or causal induction and extrapolation which we considered on page 111, and by which the presentation of an M can justify us in inferring that there exists an (unperceived) P in the relation R to it. On the latter principles we can equally well predict the occurrence of a sensation in a future region of the stream of experience or hypothesize the existence of an object wholly outside the stream of experience. That this is true, however, and just how either reference works in detail, are topics which cannot well be argued in this monograph.

The question of the ultimate place and *modus operandi* of perception and the question of the existence and knowability of the external world are problems in speculative or material theory of knowledge, which is a branch of metaphysics, and illustrate therefore the pertinence of induction to the whole of philosophy. As there is no logical chasm between the sciences, or between science and common sense, so there is none between any of these and valid ontology. Much of philosophy, like much of science, is analysis and clarification of concepts; but philosophic genius consists still more, perhaps, in a power of self-conscious and contrite research into the larger affairs of existence in accordance with the logic of induction. Our doctrine then is more likely than previous devices to put philosophy at last 'on the sure

path of a science'. Philosophy will then use not only the method
but the material results of the special sciences, and may be more
'scientific' than they, not only because the gamut of the evidence it acknowledges and the scope of the hypotheses which it
promulgates are so much greater, but also because the philosopher's grasp of the logical principles of the trade may be more
complete and explicit than the ordinary scientist's.

In being germane to the researches of philosophy, the logic of
induction has jurisdiction over researches into the stuff and order
and extent of the universe, and the nature, place, origin, and
destiny of the mind. It must be the arbiter for any attempt to
ascertain the total and final nature of the world, and hence for
the moral and religious orientation of human life to its ultimate
environment, because whatever may be the nature of the world,
it must, with logical necessity, be conformable to the logic of
induction — this is no more than is contained in the bare assertion that there is a *logic* of induction. A logic of induction,
without presupposition or limitation, does not beg the question
in favor of any one metaphysics, but must be exactly as cogent
in an atheistic world as in a theistic, in Hegel's universe as in
Haeckel's. Only in conjunction with the actual evidence can
logic, deductive or inductive, decide among such hypotheses,
and only for this reason can it decide.[3]

Specifically, the applicability of the logic of induction requires
only that its objects, the Ms, shall be members of classes, and
this is no abridgment because an analysis of what it means *to be*
at all shows that it involves being a member of classes. Any
object, mental or physical, quantitative or qualitative, abstract
or concrete, temporal or eternal, an absolute atom, a flux, a flash,
or a field, a spirit or an idea, a god or a stone, is eligible then to
be an object of induction. The frequent allegations that inductive intelligence and the scientific method are pertinent only to

[3] It is a nice question whether logic, including the principle of induction,
is 'prior' to metaphysics or is the simplest part of *a priori* metaphysics. It
makes no difference for our purposes, however, and we should be ill-advised
to bait the nominalist and conventionalist with the latter proposal.

what is physical, or what is measurable, or what is mechanical, or what is atomic, allegations too often proffered by persons who do not even pretend to understand the nature of induction otherwise, are without basis. The Platonist and the pragmatist are as wrong that induction is special to the study of process and becoming as Bergson was that it is limited to the fixed and static.

To say that the validity of induction requires of the world which it explores only that it be *at least* a lattice of classes does not mean that it requires that the world be *at most* a lattice of classes. Induction is universally and necessarily valid because any possible world, even a world of utter monads, must be at least a lattice of classes, but no possible world could be only a lattice of classes, a statistical mosaic. It must have some other and more distinctive properties, and just those other properties are what, by means of the logical lattice, induction can discover.

Even the poor minimum of the logical lattice, be it observed, is somewhat more than appears in our abstract terminology of properties and groups, which to the neophyte and the semanticist are little more than a scaffolding of symbols. The classes we dwell on are not figments of a scholar's playing board, not conventions or constructions, but are the total plural being, the concrete diaspora, of those objects and events which exemplify the respective properties, solid and four-square in their several times and places. The law of large numbers, the ground and motif of the statistical mosaic, is itself a genuine nexus and interpenetration binding together class and class and the whole of things in a net so intricate and intimate that it balks the imagination and like the atmosphere almost compels us to the pretense that it is not there at all.

Just how much regularity, connection, and continuity exist in addition to the inevitable minimum of the logical lattice, is a problem for empirical research, and there is nothing in our logical thesis to beg the question in favor of either extreme atomism (the cinematograph view, for example), or extreme organicism, or anything in between. It not only is possible, but is quite likely on the prevalent evidence, as we commented in

Chapter 5, that there is a good deal of uniformity and regularity in nature, and indeed a veritable hierarchy of functional laws which, within limits, appears closer and more inclusive as we analyze nature more deeply. More than that, there is nothing in our philosophy to deny, and there is some good empirical reason to assert, that the regularity of things is carried not by a machine of harsh and static atoms but by an organization of fluid pattern. The world may even be as vital and tempestuous as the idealist or contextualist says. As it would be an absurd error to interpret our logic of determinate classes, which means only that every entity is the sort of entity it is, as though it meant that every entity is an isolated atom, so it would be absurd to interpret our logical eternalism on page 155, which means only that what is the case is the case, as if it entailed *what* is the case in such wise as to preclude 'taking time seriously' in any degree warranted by the data. The world must in fact have at least as much richness, tightness, texture, and action as occur within our experience: the processes of living and dying, the shine of colors, the smash of explosions, the flow of rivers or of emotions. The toughness, quickness, and thickness, the actual particular do and go of things, the rush of experience, solid and vivid with commingled novelty and decorum, are the very source of our ordinary notion of fatality and inexorability, far more poignant for most persons than a logical entailment. There is growing inductive reason to extrapolate from this, and to believe the rest of the universe as exuberantly active and connected as this visible sample, a fandango of events and organization. But like Gallio the inductive principle can hold the judgment seat because it cares for none of these things.

A philosophical concept, or any other concept, is an inductive hypothesis to the extent that its construction and prevalence are motivated by a belief that it is generally applicable, and every specific application of it is an overtly inductive conclusion. This is notably true of famous 'categories' such as the twin ideas of cause and substance. Induction does not depend upon either of them, but it can assess and employ them. The minimum content of the causal idea is the kind of relation and regularity which we described on page 108. How far it is worth keeping, and what additions or subtractions are profitable, will be determined by empirical confirmation. My own prediction is that men will always find it, or something like it, well nigh indispensable. Whereas the idea of cause represents a sequential regularity in the timewise stringing out of abstract events, the coördinate idea of substance represents primarily a spacewise regularity in the lumping of properties. "This is a brown pencil", for example, involves the inductive prediction that since all the segments of this space-time tube have been suffused with pencilish and brownish properties, there will be further segments similarly suffused; but the pencilish property itself is complex, concrete and profound at every instant, and consists of many properties inductively known to accompany each other generally in a 'real kind'.

In some respects we have weakened the credit of our inductive theory and sown the dragon's teeth of new conflict by our hearty assurance that our principle is competent to the uses of philosophy. As an act of caution let us interpolate that there is no compulsion on a person who accepts our theory for the purposes of science and common sense to accept it also for metaphysics — he will otherwise only be arbitrarily fencing himself out from knowledge which he might have cultivated. Among the critics affronted by the statement that induction can answer metaphysical questions, we may neglect those who simply prefer to define the word "metaphysics" so that it stands expressly for some kind of non-inductive knowledge. We can pass over also the positivists and pragmatists who assert that what metaphysicians proffer as sentences are meaningless, for although I think they are mostly wrong, if they are right it is no detriment to induction that it cannot confirm propositions which do not exist. There remain the dissidents who believe that even though metaphysical truth concerning the primitive substance and structure of the world should exist, it must lie outside the province of the principle which we have enlisted. One professed reason for the last objection is that inductive probabilities, granted their validity generally, are valid only within the train and stream of experience. To answer this it should suffice that it is an allegation of a presupposition which in fact did not occur anywhere in the development of our inductive principle. Our principle could be and was given in wholly abstract and general terms, with no reference to the diremption between the experienced and the unexperienced, any more than to that between the Presbyterian and the non-Presbyterian, and required only the distinction between a subgroup and the population in which it is included. *Ipso facto*, then, the principle can vindicate any inference from the composition of a species *MQ* to the composition of its genus, irrespective of whether both the genus and the species are experienced, or both unexperienced, or one experienced and the other not. Our only allusion to 'experience' occurs in the epistemological application, and then only in the truism that since we can actually infer only from premises which we know to be true, it seems plausible that we must ultimately rely upon an experienced *sample*. Even this, however, which is not a part of the logic of the affair, entails nothing at all concerning the character of the *population*, which may be anything whatever. An experienced species of a genus is as much a species of it as any other part of it, and the unexperienced part of the genus is as much a part as the experienced part is. The experienced species is peculiar in being experienced, but every species is peculiar in some respect. If inference could not discount peculiarities we could never induce at all, nor deduce either, for that matter. Our predicament in having to start with experience is relevant only when there is empirical evidence that what is experienced is very different from what is unexperienced. There is some general evidence for some general differences of that sort — although in these cases we do not surrender, but correct our inferences accordingly; there is much more evidence for far-reaching similarities. We need not condemn the pathetic preference, indulged by our humanistic brothers, for predicting what will happen to *us* rather than exploring the inner nature of things, but we cannot extend any special logical privileges to such parochialism. On some important counts, the chasm between the present and future sectors of my experience, to say nothing of other persons' experience, or 'possible' experience, is greater than that between the experienced and unexperienced regions of a wholly contemporary class. There is, in principle, no scruple against asking the ultimate nature of things in themselves which would not operate against asking what will happen to a biscuit in a hot oven.

One metaphysical department, cosmology, has been sometimes denied to be amenable to induction because its objects — God or the world, for example — are peculiar in another respect than their mere unexperiencedness: they are unique and *sui generis*, and hence not members of populations, or they are simply too big for our inductive rod to fathom. The latter idea is behind the frequent agnostic advice to delay indefinitely any cosmological conclusion because, say, 'all the evidence we have gathered in two thousand years is an infinitesimally small portion of the total facts'. The fallacy of this we have already exposed: the ratio between the bulk of the sample and the bulk of the population is not a significant factor in the probability of an induction, which a quite moderate quantum of evidence can peg at a level that no further accumulation could much surpass. If there is reason to think that the universe still conceals prodigious secrets from us — an easily disputable proposition — this is not the mere negative fact that there is so much of it which we have not observed, but the affirmative fact that what we have observed contains inductive indications of crucial differences beyond. The other objection to inductive cosmology does not treat the universe as a population too bloated for our samples to represent, but treats it as a single individual supposed to have no property which our data can share, and hence to be unlinked to our evidence by any middle term M. It is logically impossible, however, for the cosmos or anything else either to have no properties at all or to have none which is shared with other things, including our experience. Genuine uniqueness, in fact, and particularly the kind of uniqueness attributed to God or the universe, consists in extreme richness of character, and hence in having many properties and belonging to many classes, and is the best possible guaranty that the object which possesses it will be inductively accessible by countless approaches.

Perhaps the warmest opponents of the proposition that induction can discover metaphysical truth are those philosophers who are anxious for the prerogatives of what they suppose to be peculiarly metaphysical organs — intuition, pure reason, insight, and the rest. I do not think that there are any non-inductive organs, beyond analytic reason and observation reports, but we may be assured that if there are, they can interpose no bar to the coöperative judgment of induction and even of induction from sense experience. Our inductive philosophy is the indispensable check, therefore, on the recklessness which goes beyond the warrant of the evidence as well as on the skepticism which refuses to go as far.

The proponents of the more mystical varieties of knowledge leave unclear, along with so much else, whether they intend to assert that only non-inductive faculties are valid in metaphysics and morals, or merely that non-inductive faculties are valid there too. By the same token, they do not explain whether they would advance their peculiar revelations as a substitute for inductive inference and conclusions, or merely wish them to be accepted as inductive premises on a par with the deliverances of sense experience.

Logically, we know, there is no reason why induction or scientific method must, as is often charged, take its start from 'sense' data. Just as the population M may consist of anything, experienced or unexperienced, so the sample MQ, although if it is to provide an ultimate datum for inference it must be in some wise experienced, may be experienced in any mode which in fact nature has vouchsafed to us. Whether there are other modes of 'experiencing' than 'sensation' is a question for semantics and psychophysics: for semantics, because there are yet no clear independent definitions of "experience" and "sensation", and for psychophysics because it is the study which should determine what the content and conditions of mental life actually are. I suspect that on the clearest and most profitable interpretations of the words it will be found that all 'experience' is 'sensory', but our philosophy of induction is quite indifferent to this result. If there are non-sensory data they must be members of classes, and that is all that is needed for the inductive principle to operate on them.

It is very important to notice, however, that whether or not there are non-sensory data, or even transcendent insights which somehow by-pass the inductive procedure, there certainly exist, in the same logical universe, sensory data, and there certainly are valid inductive conclusions from those data. The latter conclusions will always have logical authority to check superstition by opposing or amending the results either of supposedly non-sensory insights or of inductions therefrom. The deliverances of sense, everybody agrees, are uniquely stable, repeatable, inter-subjective, capable of being corroborated and assisted by instruments, and hence are reliable evidences for highly probable inductions and confirmations in ways in which the other forms of experience, if such there be, admittedly are not. No non-sensory or non-inductive conclusion can legitimately stand against a sensory-inductive proposition when the two are opposed, while if they are not opposed the non-sensory or non-inductive revelation has generally contributed little or nothing to the result. There remains, apparently, the possibility that the non-inductive result, without conflicting with any sensory-inductive result, simply 'goes beyond it', revealing extra truths to which the latter is neutral or irrelevant. This may be logically conceivable, though I have been unable to imagine a situation in which the possibility would be realized, but in the present state of our knowledge it is exceedingly incredible. The mystics themselves are fond of comparing their insights to another sense than the normal equipment, and of drawing an analogy between their advantage and the advantage which a seeing man has over a blind man, and this very figure condemns them. Our ordinary senses inductively confirm or disconfirm each other's results. Although the blind man's knowledge of the world is less generously decorated with 'raw feels' (in E. C. Tolman's phrase) than the ordinary man's, it may be no less extensive and exact than the latter's. The world is so knit that whether we get our data from one sense or from sixty we should and do arrive inductively at the same probable diagram of it. Without far more solid and consilient effect than the mystics and intuitionists have achieved so far, the very fact that any of their results 'goes beyond', that is, is not corroborated by, induction from sense experience, is fairly conclusive evidence *against* it.

In short, to prove that induction is a logically valid avenue to knowledge in every area is not, I grant, to prove that there is no other avenue, in one area or another, but it is to prove that there is nothing knowable by any avenue which is not in principle knowable by induction too. Lalande and Reichenbach go too far, I fear, in averring that induction alone 'can prove the authenticity even of revelation' or of clairvoyance.[4] The champion of revelation or of clairvoyance would retort that although only induction can prove its authenticity to the partisans of induction, to him it proves itself. As a matter of public policy, however, we should do well to discipline the proponents of non-inductive methods — revelation, clairvoyance, authority, tradition, intuition, insight, feeling, synthetic *a priori* judgments, or dianoetical intellection — by enforcing the rule of discourse that no proposition be admitted to serious philosophic attention, whatever its non-inductive boasts, unless and until it can approve itself also by induction, *und zwar* by induction from sense data. This would discourage not only the patrons of instinct and fanaticism but the almost equally irresponsible parties of traditionalists who appeal to 'Reason' as an excuse for professing attractive propositions for which there are no *reasons*.

[4] The phrase is from André Lalande, *Les Théories de l'Induction et de l'Expérimentation* (Paris, 1929), p. 261. The allusions to clairvoyance are Reichenbach's: e.g., *Erkenntnis*, Vol. VI (1936), p. 34.

We have ourselves at least tentatively admitted just two kinds of non-inductive knowledge: immediate apprehension of particular events, and the acceptance of the results of logical analysis, whether the latter be tautologies or eternal truths. That such knowledges occur seems to me a plain fact of immediate experience; that their occurrence is required for the working of induction appears to me a sound epistemological conclusion. By a direct apprehension of particular events we establish the ultimate premises of induction; by logical analysis of abstract connections of meanings we establish the validity of the passage from premise to conclusion. Sensory apprehension and logical understanding, however, if they exist, are not exceptions to our rule that whatever non-inductive forms of knowledge there may be, their objects are amenable also to induction. *I feel hot* and *Twice two is four* may not need inductive confirmation, at the moment, but they can get it. Since the principle of induction is completely general, true of all classes and their subclasses, it is true of the classes constituted by those abstract entities, principles, essences, and forms, to which analytic and logical truths are confined. Most of the analytic truths of early mathematics, for example, were discovered inductively or by experiment: that the sum of the first n odd numbers is n^2, that the square on the hypotenuse of a right triangle equals the sum of the squares on the other two sides, that a circle encloses a greater area than any other figure of equal periphery. Newton is supposed to have discovered the binomial theorem, so essential to our present theory, by observing that all the numbers on which he tested it conformed to it. Later, to be sure, either conceptual analysis has made the conclusion intuitively self-evident, or a series of analyses have enabled its deduction, step by intuitive step, from premises which are intuitively self-evident. In the meantime, however, the inductive evidence had given a genuinely valid though inconclusive support to the proposition, and it is doubtful to this day how many discoveries in logic or mathematics are not induced first and deduced or analytically intuited only afterward. The primitive propositions of mathematical systems are still held, in many cases, simply because acceptable results follow from them — in other words, they are held as confirmed hypotheses.[5] There can be no valid objection to helping out, in such operations, the faltering scalpel of analysis with the crudely effective handax of induction. This device, which I would call "dialectical induction", has innumerable uses, in philosophy and outside of it; it is a genuinely 'mathematical induction' in contrast with the deductive procedure usually called by that name. Because some inductively warranted propositions turned out to be analytic and necessary, it was easy for the rationalists to conclude, falsely I am sure, that if we only sharpened our wits sufficiently we should find all true propositions to be necessary. Because any necessary proposition is bound to be confirmed inductively by every observable instance, it was natural enough for J. S. Mill to draw the equally false inference that supposedly necessary propositions just are unexceptionably confirmed empirical generalizations. The principle of dialectical induction, of respect for convergent evidence and inductive good sense even in logic, is the justification of the notorious Anglo-Saxon distrust of demonstration and the doctrinaire. Conversely, I think, one reason why so much of the recent philosophy of science and logic has been less free and fruitful than it need have been is its reluctance to confess to dialectical induction. Despising the embryonic stage of large hypotheses, consilient evidences, and inductive probabilities, it has tried to leap from a standing start to apodeictic proof and transparent identities.

The principle of induction itself, provable *a priori*, gets a massive and for many persons more impressive vindication as an object of induction and hypothesis, a vast confluence of testimony with a solider impact on the solar plexus than any thesis of arithmetic. The most obvious evidence for the induc-

[5] See Bertrand Russell, *An Inquiry into Meaning and Truth* (New York, 1940), p. 16. So N. R. Campbell can reverse an old dictum of Russell's, and declare that many so-called 'deductions' are only disguised inductions. (Cited by Jeffreys, *Theory of Probability*, p. 6.)

tive principle we have observed in the empirical law of large numbers, that induction works, its conclusions are often true. (To be exact, almost the only unmistakable instances of inductions with true conclusions are provided by dialectical inductions in the development of the mathematical sciences. A strictly empirical generalization is seldom or never completely verified, but is only further confirmed by a more extended sampling; an induction like the one about the sums of the odd numbers, however, is later verified by a demonstration.) More broadly and complexly, our theory of induction is solidly confirmed by methods of hypothesis. Even our 'proof' of the logical law of large numbers, in Chapter 4, although it can be readily completed with an analytic demonstration, depended mostly on illustrative instances, inductively persuasive. In the large, our principle is confirmed by such considerations as that to deny it is to acquiesce in incredible coincidences. It is inductively absurd that a theory should come so near and yet miss; that so fundamental a logical truth as the law of large numbers should so exactly correspond to the laws of animal docility and to the discriminations of trained scientific judgment, and yet that, so far as the validity of induction is concerned, the subclasses of any class might as well be predominantly *unlike* the class in their statistical composition.

8

ALTERNATIVES AND ANTICIPATIONS

While we discussed the sources of the validity of inductive inference and tried to dissipate some of the misunderstandings which cloud its title, we have had occasionally to make at least sidelong allusions to whole rival philosophies of induction. There is a hint in this that however affirmative and constructive the purpose of this essay, it would be better understood and its validity more fairly appraised, to say nothing of the whole problem's being better appreciated, if we proceeded now to size it up alongside similar and competing accounts. Since theories of induction, although not much noticed by the ordinary run of philosophers, logicians, and scientists, are numerous and intricate, the carrying out of that enterprise here would almost double the bulk of this volume, and is impracticable. We can, however, and ought to, sketch out roughly the status of the philosophy of induction by identifying at least the principal kinds of theory which divide the field. I am the more willing to describe them, it may be surmised, because on the whole they seem the kind of 'good errors' into which one would expect well-disposed philosophers to be trapped if induction were in fact valid on the principle which we have defended.

Theories of induction are most instructively classified according to their treatment of the two connections most important in the inductive situation: the connection between the subject and predicate characters, M and P, and the connection between the compositions of the sample and of the population, $\frac{[MQP]}{[MQ]}$ and $\frac{[MP]}{[M]}$. If there is any validity in the process by which we conclude to the existence of a law, universal or statistical, at least one of these connections must be not mere material concomitance but a logical implication, either a demonstrative entailment or an intermediate but objective probability.

Hume, we observed, declared that neither of these crucial connections is logically implicative at all, certain or probable, and hosts of neo-Humeans· today, including positivists, 'analysts', pragmatists, and adherents to several affiliated philosophies of science, are following the master in the two oddly matched articles, that there is and can be no logic of induction, and yet that it is somehow incumbent on the right kind of man to submit himself to the *de facto* canons of the inductive sciences. Some of them have worked out exquisite and studied codifications of the canons, far surpassing Hume's loose handful of 'rules by which to judge of causes and effects',[1] but they have done little or nothing which affects the original principles. Calling the logical problem of induction 'meaningless' or 'unreal', to palliate the absence of a solution, they justify induction biologically and anthropologically, as animal faith or problem solving: it is a vital urge; we can't help it; it is a going concern; it works; it is a convention; it is a practical demand; it is our best because it is our only chance. A few more boldly but more providently suggest that induction is safe because its predictions can actually create the facts of which they treat, either by sheer wishing, or by believing, or by definition, or because 'reality' for all practical purposes *is* what induction eventually declares it to be. Others more modestly contend that induction is safe because it makes no predictions — an inductive

[1] *Treatise*, Bk. I, Pt. III, sec. 15. To illustrate the wide variety of the neo-Humean philosophy, it must suffice to name Wittgenstein's and Dewey's works, previously cited, A. J. Ayer, *Language, Truth, and Logic* (London, 1936), and F. Kaufmann, *The Methodology of the Social Sciences* (New York, 1944).

hypothesis is simply the current record of observations to date, to be rejected or modified when different observations occur. Essentially, however, all the parties in this school agree, when we come down to everyday cases, that the fact, for example, that the bell has rung when the button was pressed in the past is no *reason* whatever for the normal prediction that it will ring next time the button is pressed.

Like Hume's, the program of this school is rather reassuring to us than otherwise, because like his it depends mostly on the eminently refutable doctrine that where there is not a demonstrative entailment or inconsistency, but there is a natural propensity to believe, there can be no logical connection at all. To this the neo-Humeans are able to add one or both of two more modern grounds, the pragmatic theory that all logical principles are rules of inquiry whose validity depends on their empirical corroboration, and the 'frequency theory', that 'probability' is always a limiting frequency in an endless series of trials. Since both the empirical success of logical principles and the limiting frequency in a statistical series must be established by induction, either theory leaves induction wholly unsupported; but that the theories are far from foregone conclusions we have already remarked. We have also remarked on the double anomaly of maintaining the inductive standards while denying that induction is logically valid: first, and obviously, because the denial leaves our adherence to the standards with no excuse except habit or caprice; secondly, and less obviously, because so long as we do adhere to the inductive standards, either with or without reason, the principle of dialectical induction, operating on the patent facts of the situation, should impel us to the conclusion that induction must be logically valid after all, because the opposite conclusion, that our loyalty to induction is mere habit or caprice, is inductively absurd. The person who rejects induction in practice as well as in principle can be affected only by an *a priori* analysis. The person who accepts it in practice, however, stultifies himself if he rejects it in principle, because he thereby violates his own canons — for

he accepts the unacceptable hypothesis that the immense successes of the inductive organon, its intricate and exact development and apparent validation at the hands of non-Humean
logicians, and the sacrificial devotion to it even of the Humeans,
are a logically irrelevant chapter of accidents; that the age-old
apprehension of both scientists and laymen that a well-confirmed
induction has very much the same kind and almost the same
amount of objective credibility as a valid deduction, which
the non-Humean hypothesis explains and justifies, is entirely
delusory.

In its negative conclusion the Humean philosophy of induction
directly contravenes our own, although its premises show themselves so vulnerable that it poses no dreadful obstacle. Most
philosophers, on the other hand, take for granted that induction
is valid, albeit without adhering to any definite theory of it.
Questioned, they refer vaguely to 'sufficient reason', 'causation',
or 'uniformity'. Back of this foreground of placid acceptance,
however, there are a number of comparatively firm and professional theories which explicitly have tried to justify induction
with terms like those. The affirmative theories are not inconsistent with our theory or with each other, and if valid would
presumably augment the credibility provided by each other and
by our theory. As fundamental principles, however, I think
they are not valid.

Among the affirmative theories we may distinguish first those
which assert, in spite of Hume, that there is a direct necessitat-
ing connection between the inductive subject and predicate,
M and P, which can be recognized immediately and intuitively
without the bother of sampling. Now, if this power, efficacy,
or fitness is less than a logical implication, demonstrative or
probable, it is a mere extra concomitant whose association with
M and P is a further empirical fact to be discovered and confirmed by induction, and it does nothing to justify induction.
That it actually involves an entailment, however, has been
maintained in the Aristotelian doctrine of 'scientific' and
'essential' propositions, in the schools of medieval and ration-

alistic philosophy which merged or confounded the notions of cause and effect and of ground and consequent, and in recent theories of synthetic *a priori* propositions defended by the Cambridge philosophers of common sense.[2] The idea of a necessary connection between M and P we cannot reject out of hand: we have admitted some necessary propositions (like *All parrots are birds*), and it is not at all easy to say what is the difference between a 'synthetic' and an 'analytic' proposition in any but the crudest cases. It can be affirmed, however, that the necessitarian school claim necessity for far more propositions than have it, but that even so they do not dare claim necessity for all the generalizations required by common sense and science. Certainly — and this is a consideration of which the school have been generally too negligent — they cannot claim that we actually *intuit* a necessity on each of those occasions, and an unintuited necessity, or a mere general assurance that there must be necessary connections 'underlying' the phenomenal state of affairs, is quite worthless to justify any particular induction and hence to justify induction in general. The theory of necessary connection is even more conspicuously unable to account for statistical inductions, which are usually more important to science and common sense than universal ones, and so leaves us without any reason to expect crows to be black or stoves to cook food. If the theory can be adjusted to the uses of statistics it must be so by the ampler notion, proposed by some advocates of organicism and contextualism, that there may be intrinsic relations of graded 'tendency' or probability between M and P. This has been too little elaborated to be fairly judged. In any event, however, the theory would not account for inductions in artificial and arbitrary situations, like our bagful of

[2] See, for example, G. F. Stout and A. C. Ewing, in the *Aristotelian Society Supplementary Volume XIV* (London, 1935), pp. 47–49 and 66. Compare also pp. 121–22 above, and the references there. Galileo was not the last great scientist to believe that when once the correlated characters of nature are found by analytic attention, their correlation stands out as intrinsic and necessary.

marbles, where no conceivable insight could discern without sampling the prevalent tendency-connection between being-a-marble-in-the-bag and being-red.

The other affirmative theories of induction assert, with us, and in spite of Hume again, that there is a connection, either of entailment or of probability, between the composition of the sample and the composition of the population. Since it is clearly false empirically, and indeed contradictory logically, that from the composition of just any sample we must be able to deduce the population composition, the entailment school is limited to those who, like Bacon, Mill, and Joseph, rely on a supreme premise concerning the uniformity of nature, and demand then that the sample be so cannily chosen as to rule out, by elimination, every predicate for M except P (or every subject for P except M).[3] This is the principle of Mill's famous 'methods of induction', which we noted in Chapter 5 to have ancillary value both in science and in common sense. Since the principle of uniformity, however, as Mill agreed, must be established by sampling, and since the eliminative process is never complete, this method cannot yield a fundamental philosophy of the subject, and like so many theories it lends no assistance to statistical induction at all.

Much more plausible and promising are those remaining theories which, like ours, are content with a probability implication between the composition of the sample and the composition of the population (or between the composition of the sample and the characterization of some one further member of the population). The most important and thoroughly developed, what may be called the standard logical doctrine on the subject, is the one assumed in the derivation of Laplace's rule of succession

[3] Anyone not familiar with this scheme, but curious about it, will find good critical accounts in R. M. Eaton, *General Logic* (New York, 1931), pp. 503 ff., and in C. D. Broad, "Hr. Von Wright on the Logic of Induction (I)", *Mind*, Vol. LIII (1944), pp. 13 ff. Broad's articles are a valuable survey of inductive theories, on a plan similar to our present one, though with a different conclusion.

mentioned on page 159. This accepts the classic theory of probability in a form equivalent to ours but differs by tackling the problem of induction as one in inverse probabilities. A calculation of 'inverse probability', or more accurately an 'inverse calculation' of probability, is a deduction of the probability of p in relation to q from a knowledge of the probability of q in relation to p. We observed in Chapter 4 that Bernoulli's principle yields directly the probability, given a population with a certain composition, that a sample selected from it will have a certain composition (say the same composition). We noted also that this seems to be just the inverse of what is required by the problem of induction, which is to calculate the probability, given a sample with a certain composition, that the population from which it was selected has a certain composition (say the same composition). We met this discrepancy head-on by reducing the two questions to the common factor, the question whether the sample matches the population, which is the same as the question whether the population matches the sample, and concluding that since, whatever the population may be, most of the possible samples must match the population, there is a direct, if indefinite, probability of at least so-and-so that the given sample and population match each other. The procedure not only results in a direct probability, but takes no explicit account, so far, of the 'possible' compositions of the population, or of the actual composition of the sample, the latter being considered only at the final stage, when the *a priori* inductive principle is applied to the particular occasion. The more usual approach, however, has been more meticulous, an 'inverting' of Bernoulli's theorem. The crudest inversion consists in flatly equating the probability (required for induction) that, given a sample of composition c, the population has the composition c, with the probability (yielded directly by Bernoulli's principle) that, given a population of composition c, the sample will have composition c. This in effect is what was done by older statisticians who filled in the observed values of $\dfrac{[MQP]}{[MQ]}$ and $\dfrac{[MQ\bar{P}]}{[MQ]}$

instead of the unobservable $\frac{[MP]}{[M]}$ and $\frac{[M\bar{P}]}{[M]}$ required by the fundamental sampling formula on page 86. It is the only visible support, likewise, of some more recent schools of statistical sampling theory who express the direct Bernoullian relation in such terms as "fiducial probability", "likelihood", and "confidence levels", although, since these parties are prone to accept the frequency theory of probability, their canons, eminently useful no doubt in their profession, can hardly be more than Humean convention anyhow.[4] For intermediate compositions the results of this dodge will not differ widely from our own, but it seems to have no other philosophical justification. Among its disabilities, aside from the main paradox that it begs the question whether the sample and the population match, is that when all *MQ* is *P* or no *MQ* is *P* it entails that the population *must* match.

The older, more complicated and ingratiating, inverse methods do not baldly substitute the direct for the inverse probability but conscientiously reason from one to the other by means of one of the classic inverse-probability theorems, particularly by some variant of the rule of Bayes which we described on page 113:

$$\vdash: r/pq = \frac{r/p \times q/pr}{q/p}.$$

If we take *q* to be our sample, with composition *c*, and *r* to be the inductive hypothesis that the population has composition *c*, and *p*, as before, to be the rest of our knowledge, this rule, and others equivalent to it, will — on certain assumptions — yield Laplace's rules of succession, both the useless one given on page 159 and the more useful and familiar one, that the probability that any one further *M* will be *P* is equal to $\frac{[MQP] + 1}{[MQ] + 2}$, and they will yield also a conclusion

[4] For the old standard procedure, see for example H. E. Garrett, *Statistics in Psychology and Education* (New York, 1926), Chapter 3. For the newer prescriptions, and an extended bibliography, see S. S. Wilks, *Mathematical Statistics* (Princeton, 1943).

to the effect that the population very probably has very nearly
the composition c. The form in which it gives the latter result,
and the main principles involved in the process, are not very
different from ours. There are serious anomalies and insuffi-
ciencies in some of its results, however, and even greater
anomalies in the principal assumption required, namely, that
a priori, in the absence of any inductive evidence, the population
is as likely to have one composition as another — that 'all possible compositions are equally probable'. Not the least of the
virtues of our own doctrine is that, avoiding the inverse method,
it avoids also the stipulation of equal *a priori* probabilities for
possible compositions, and indeed of any *a priori* probabilities
for them at all, 'the greatest stumbling-block in the theory
of probability'.[5]

Although some adherents to the inverse principle have been
well enough content with its unaided results, others, or the same
ones at other times, have written that with or without the
questionable assumption of equiprobable population compositions it needs to be assisted by powerful material principles
analogous to Mill's uniformity of nature if it is to do the job
required. In particular, they have held, it cannot establish a
respectable probability for a universal generalization unless it
is fortified by a principle of 'limitation of independent variety'
— that the properties of the world are bunched or bundled in a
finite number of groups (real kinds) such that all the properties
in any one group are universally associated with all the others

---

[5] The phrase is from Jeffreys, *Scientific Inference* (New York and Cambridge, 1931), p. 20. Jeffreys nevertheless develops and defends the inverse
method in that work and in his *Theory of Probability*, Chapter 3. C. D.
Broad explains it thoroughly, and attacks it on the ground indicated, in
"The Principles of Problematic Induction", *Proceedings of the Aristotelian
Society*, Vol. XXVIII (1928), pp. 1–46. Broad defends it again, however,
in *Mind*, Vol. LIII (1944), pp. 97 ff., as valid *if* the classic theory of probability is valid, which he now disputes. R. Carnap utilizes very much the
same scheme, including equal prior probabilities, in terms of the *Spielraum*
theory, "On Inductive Logic", *Philosophy of Science*, Vol. XII (1945),
pp. 72 ff.

in that group.[6] Since this principle itself would have to be established by sampling and since it would be harder to establish than less grandiose generalizations, and since it could in any case contribute nothing to the confirmation of merely statistical inductions, it clearly cannot be expected to provide part of the ultimate basis of inductive validity, though it may sometimes furnish a useful increment to inductive probabilities already established by austerely logical methods.

It is possible, of course, that induction should eventually be vindicated by some other and perhaps more powerful theory of probability than ours, but nothing very effective has so far been developed in that direction. Keynes and Broad, whose principles ostensibly are hospitable to other than statistical probabilities, appealed to the idea of 'analogy' to help out inverse probability and the limitation principle, but they did not systematically collate it with their other formulas and they left its contribution very obscure. Carnap has explicitly revised the law of succession to take account of points of similarity as well as the mere number of the sample, and it is quite likely that our own somewhat crude principle of analogy on page 113 can be bettered by his or similar methods, but it is not at all likely that this will affect the cardinal principle of our inductive philosophy. Much more revolutionary departures in probability theory are the articles of organicists like Bosanquet and Whitehead, who eschew class ratios of any sort in favor of a primordial intuitable 'fitness' — a fitness either of the inductive predicate P to the inductive subject M, or of the inductive conclusion to the inductive premise.[7] Their results have hardly been definite enough to provide a solution of our problem or even to make clear the nature of the nexus which they prescribe. The only 'fitness'

[6] This doctrine, widely received among philosophical logicians and logical philosophers, was worked out by J. M. Keynes, *Treatise*, Part III, and by C. D. Broad (e.g., in the *Aristotelian Society* address cited above).

[7] See A. N. Whitehead, *Process and Reality* (New York, 1929), pp. 303–316; B. Bosanquet, *Implication and Linear Inference* (London, 1920). The *Gestalt*-psychologists' theory of 'closure' may be similarly used.

which I am able to perceive or to conceive, in process or reality, meantime, is the *de facto* regularity and interfusion which, we noted in the preceding chapter, must be discovered *by* induction.

Along the fringes of more explicit theories of induction there are some doctrines too equivocal or inchoate to be classifiable with any conviction. Frequently intimated, for example, is the idea that the inductive connection is ultimate, a separate and primitive kind of 'reasonableness', coördinate with but different from the deductive connection, either demonstrative or probable. This, however, is surely an unstable position. Either it will disclose itself as a euphemistic way of expressing the Humean view that induction has no logical validity but is merely an inveterate animal habit elaborated by our culture circle into an exacting ritual, or it will find itself pressed to disclose the common logical feature which entitles induction to be called "reasonable" along with deduction, and hence must resort to an analysis like ours.

A somewhat obscure principle, again, which has been often alleged as an endorsement of induction, from Peirce to Dewey and Lewis, is that induction in the long run is 'self-correcting' — "This is the marvel of it", cried Peirce.[8] If this means, however, that inductions persevered in, and adjusted to the change of evidence, must eventually come right, we know it is false. If it means that they probably will come right, it is true, but this truth follows only from some prior inductive theory like ours and cannot provide an inductive theory by itself.

It would have been a welcome task for me to present a more hopeful report on rival theories of the justification of induction. Other things equal, the more strings there are to the inductive bow, the better for all of us. But although the brief notice here given to the other theories is not in itself enough to refute them or even to explain them adequately, I fear that the more carefully they are examined the more evident will their incapacity appear, in approximately the respects which I have mentioned. Our gain will have been that in clarifying the faults of other

[8] See *Collected Papers*, II, p. 456.

justifications of induction we come to see more clearly the elements of the problem and hence the capacities of our own theory.

It would be an even more welcome task now to name an array of logicians and philosophers who adhere to the inductive theory which I have presented. Unfortunately, no such array exists. In a vague way, all men, and especially all scientists and philosophers, have normally spoken and acted as if they accepted a doctrine like this, but they have not stated it except by innuendo, and if it is present in their works it is present somewhat as the statue is present in the block of marble. The account which I have defended, however, has especially near affinities with many statistical methods and with several philosophic theories.

I cannot claim C. I. Lewis as a devotee of our whole theory, but I find in the last two chapters of his *Mind and the World-Order* almost a definitive statement of the conditions which must be fulfilled by a tenable theory of the probability of induction. His teaching there is that induction must be warranted by a probability connection, that a probability connection is analytic and necessary, objective and independent of opinion and inclination, yet differing from logical implication just in that its consequent may be false though its antecedent is true, and that, taking its premises from the indefeasible given, induction must accordingly be valid in any conceivable world, uniform or chaotic, demonic, dionysian, or mechanical. Beyond this, unfortunately, he refrained from propounding either a specific account of probability or a demonstration that induction has such a probability, and I am not counting on his alliance in either of these connections.

From a different direction, without much epistemological forethought, writers on statistics have long been accustomed to employ with ingenious facility various *a priori* laws of large numbers generally equivalent to ours, and textbooks of statistics are fat with sampling formulas similar to the one of which we make so much. At least one important text, logically more sophisticated than most, *An Introduction to the Theory of Statistics* by Yule and Kendall, solves our problem almost inadvertently by pointing out that the least favorable value of the standard error of sampling occurs when the population is assumed to be divided half and half between P and *non-P*.[9] In fine, common statistical rule of thumb is in nearly perfect accord with our theory, and most of what is said and done by statisticians and scientists conforms closely to our recommendations though their explanations and logical defense are seldom valid. Our use of the rule of arithmetical combinations to count 'protosamples' is a fairly familiar operation among those concerned with statistics and probability, and may appear for example at one stage of the development of Laplace's rules of succession. Jeffreys indeed uses it for a general proof that a matching sample is the most probable, though he at once throws the advantage away by compounding the idea with the inverse principle.[10] There are miscellaneous kinds of set-theory and combinatorial analyses of probability, so far without much philosophical awareness, which may be expected to issue in our kind of solution of the inductive problem.

Among the published accounts of induction which are known to me, the one most similar to ours is by Josiah Royce. Royce, however, attributed the theory to Peirce, and it is true that it can be pieced together from *disjecta membra* to be found among Peirce's kaleidoscopic thoughts on the subject. Royce's short study came to my attention too late to be of any help, but readers of Peirce will recognize how much my discussion of probability and of induction owes to him, both in detail and in some of its largest themes. Peirce is a coruscating sun whose darkest spots are usually brighter than the orbs of other lumi-

[9] G. U. Yule and M. G. Kendall (London, 1937), p. 354. The authors however at once recommend the filling in of the error formula with the values found for the composition of the sample, in the manner which we described on pp. 190–91 as simple inversion of Bernoulli's theorem. Yule and Kendall are among the few statisticians who show an awareness of the apparatus of the logic of classes.

[10] See his *Scientific Inference*, pp. 25 and 27 ff.

naries. Our theory of probability, for example, appears in this passage: "The validity of an inference . . . consists in the real fact that, when premisses like those of the argument in question are true, conclusions related to them like that of this argument are also true. . . . In a logical mind an argument is always conceived as a member of a *genus* of arguments all constructed in the same way, and such that, when their premisses are real facts, their conclusions are so also. If the argument is demonstrative, then this is always so; if it is only probable, then it is for the most part so". [11] On this basis he undertakes 'to demonstrate mathematically that the validity of Induction, in the proper sense of the term, that is to say, experimental reasoning, follows, through the lemmas of probabilities, from the rudiments of the doctrine of necessary consequences, without any assumption whatever about the future being like the past, or similar results following similar conditions, or the uniformity of nature, or any such vague principle'.[12] Unfortunately, though Peirce continues, "I shall set forth the reasoning in strict accuracy of form; and I defy anybody to find a flaw in it", he nowhere fulfills this ringing promise. It is possible however to glean from him numerous intimations of our own kind of proof. We find in his writings, for example, our cardinal principle that the sample MQ can be treated as a member of a hyperpopulation of sets of the same size, included in the population M, among which the majority evince the predicate P in the same proportion as does M,[13] and hence that a large proportion of inductive conclusions must be true.[14] There occurs too the proposition that if the principle of matching samples permits inferring the composition of MQ from a knowledge of the composition of M, it permits inferring the composition of M from a knowledge of the composition of MQ, because the relation of being 'probably and approximately equal' is a 'convertible relation'.[15] More particularly, he advances the rule of 'probable error' to specify the

[11] *Collected Papers*, II, pp. 393–394. Compare p. 437.
[12] The same, p. 58.   [13] The same, pp. 438–439.
[14] The same, pp. 427, 472.   [15] The same, pp. 441, 451.

degree of probable approximation, and he points out that in the most unfavorable of cases the product

$$\frac{[MP]}{[M]} \times \frac{[M\bar{P}]}{[M]}$$

can be no greater than $\frac{1}{2} \times \frac{1}{2}$, and that the only material qualification which we need make is that we do not *know* that there is a demon interfering with our inductions.[16]

In spite of all the foregoing, however, it would be rash for me to assert that what I have advocated is the, or even a, Peircean theory. Not only does he not univocally and connectedly state it; he tantalizingly appears again and again to deny it and the main principles on which it rests. To follow his odyssey is a liberal education in our subject. It seems only a relatively minor departure, to be sure, when he demands an assurance of 'randomness' or 'fairness' of selection,[17] but by this demand, which he admits is never satisfiable,[18] he vitiates all his brave probability principles, deductive and inductive. The requirement becomes indeed a rejection of the classic theory of probability in favor of the frequency theory, which turns, of necessity, all his logical hopes of induction into moonshine. Even when he writes out the principle of the statistical syllogism, that if a bean is drawn from a bag containing white beans in the proportion $\frac{m}{n}$, there is a probability of $\frac{m}{n}$ that the bean will be white, he stipulates that the bean be 'drawn in such a way that in the long run the relative number of white beans so drawn would be equal to the relative number in the bag'.[19] It appears, then, that what we are really sampling is not the finite collection of beans in the bag, but an indefinitely 'long run' of drawings.[20] This by itself is not yet fatal because our inductive principle might work as well on a drawing-series as on the bagful of beans.

[16] The same, pp. 428, 453, 473.
[17] The same, pp. 373, 473, 487, etc.
[18] The same, p. 487.
[19] The same, p. 373.
[20] The same, pp. 405, 412–413, 501–502.

What is fatal is the next step, enjoined by the frequency theory: that the probability that we have a matching sample is defined, not by the proportion of matching sets included in the sampled population (bagful or drawing-series, as the case may be), but by the proportion of samples matching that original population which 'would be' got in a new series, a long-run series of whole sample-selections like the present one. The proportion of matching sets in the original population (bagful or drawing-series) can be known by the law of large numbers, and can hence validate an induction to the composition of the population. The number of matching selections in the new series can be known, if at all, only by induction, and is worthless to validate induction. It makes all the difference in the world, as we re-marked on page 39, whether the 'class of inferences' or 'genus of arguments' from which we compute our probability is con-stituted by the *kinds* of inferences afforded by the actual select-able sets in the population, or consists of the particular selectings and inferrings, as individual psychophysical events, which, it is storied, we should eventually make. It is fascinating, and exasperating, to watch how incessantly, over a period of many decades, Peirce seemed to be asserting the right doctrine, the fertile one, concerning the roster of 'possible inferences', and how fatally his account always slewed around into the abysmally different and sterile frequency theory.[21]

More or less explicitly aware of the contradiction between his frequency theory of probability and his hearty pretense of having solved the problem of induction, he intersperses his anticipations of our analysis with alternate paeans of despair and appeals to other and very inadequate solutions. Thus he praises the Abbé Gratry's opinion that induction prospers by grace of a divine miracle because, being 'intimately connected — as the true account should be — with a general philosophy of the universe', it is truer to the situation than 'many a pedantic

---

[21] Passages expressing one or both of the two versions of "possible in-ferences" appear in Vol. II on pp. 393, 394, 400, 401, 409, 415, 416, 432, etc., etc.

. . . juggle with probabilities'.[22] He asserts *a priori* that there is
'a manifest impossibility in so tracing out any probability for
a synthetic conclusion', and he condemns such attempts as
quackery.[23] He accordingly has sporadic resort to the sugges-
tions that the world must be metaphysically constituted in favor
of induction, that there is a pre-established harmony between
our minds and the nature of things, that inductibility is to be
guaranteed in a Kantian way as a presupposition of possible
experience, that nature evinces real connections ('habits') which
are more than factual uniformities, that scientific generalizations are timeless abstractions or tautologies, that reality is
manufactured by the totality of our inductions, and that induction is 'self-correcting', or at any rate would be so if we kept on
sampling until we exhausted the population. In one passage he
proposes a simple inversion of Bernoulli's theorem, in another he
attributes to induction a unique kind of 'trustworthiness' suggestive of recent theories of confirmation, while in his article on
'Probability' in the *Century Dictionary* he appears satisfied by
the matter-of-fact observation that the samples which men
draw generally do match their populations, — the Humean
philosophy of animal faith.[24]

[22] *Collected Papers*, II, pp. 430–431.
[23] The same, pp. 423–424, 427; p. 500. These strictures not only contradict his statement that 'the universe need have no peculiar constitution
to render ampliative inference valid' (pp. 474, 496), but match poorly
with the title which his editors, justly enough, affix to his discussion of the
subject, "On the Probability of Synthetic Inferences" (p. 427). In one or
more of these passages Peirce may be aspersing the inverse method, which
he sometimes roundly condemns both (*a*) because it presupposes the classic
theory of probability and (*b*) because it is incorrect even on that theory
(because of the difficulty about equally probable compositions). His discussion is clogged by his belief that the classic theory must treat the inductive problem as that of ascertaining in how many universes a specific
inference would be made true, instead of how many of our inferences would
be made true in this specific universe (pp. 472, 500, etc.).
[24] The student who cares to glean in this rich field of ideas will find all
the above proposed, more or less baldly, among the following pages of the
Collected Papers: Vol. II, pp. 409, 427, 431, 432, 442–443, 447, 453, 455–
456; Vol. V, pp. 162, 218, and 284.

Royce's analysis of induction, published with didactic brevity in the introductory section of his contribution to the volume of logical studies of the *Encyclopaedia of the Philosophical Sciences*,[25] much more clearly than Peirce traces the inductive principle home, as we do, to the distribution of actual proto-samples in the population. Although he still demands that the sample at hand be chosen 'fairly', he seems content to define a 'fair sample' as one not known to be unfair, and it is easy to forgive his superfluous scruples that the population be finite and of a determinate composition, since these conditions can always be fulfilled.

The object of this monograph, in summary, has been to show that inductive inference, on which depends the possibility of knowledge and virtue, and whose principles make the difference between science and superstition, is rationally valid, coherent with the rest of logic and mathematics, and universally applicable to experience and action. Since the premises of an induction clearly do not endow its conclusion with a demonstrative certainty, the attaining of our object required first that we portray a kind of logical relation which, in a precise sense, is of the same quality and texture with demonstrative entailment but susceptible of degree. This we found in 'probability', understood in a manner very similar to the classic theory of probability, which entails, if it is not equivalent to, the law of the proportional syllogism, that if $\frac{m}{n}$ of a class $\mathfrak{M}$ have the property $\mathfrak{P}$, and $\mathfrak{a}$ is a member of $\mathfrak{M}$, then there is a probability of degree $\frac{m}{n}$ that $\mathfrak{a}$ is $\mathfrak{P}$. Our proof of the validity of induction consists then in pointing out that an inductive inference from the composition of a sample MQ to the composition of its population M has a high degree of the probability thus analyzed. Specifically, let $\mathfrak{a}$ be the sample MQ, and let $\mathfrak{M}$ be the hyper-population of groups of the same size as MQ included in M, and let $\mathfrak{P}$ be the property of having approximately the same statistical composition as M with respect to a predicate P. Then it is demonstrable that, if the number $[MQ]$ is fairly large, the great

[25] Edited by Arnold Ruge, etc. (London, 1913). See pages 82–88.

majority of 𝕸 is 𝕻. Hence, since a is 𝕸, it is highly probable, by the proportional syllogism, that a is 𝕻; that is, it is highly probable that the sample matches the population. Conveniently restated, this is the inductive principle: that any considerable sample from any population is probably and approximately similar to the population (and conversely) in any specified statistical respect, the minimum degree of probability and approximation being assignable for samples of any given size by familiar statistical tables of deviation. This is an analytic law of logic *by* which, given a sample of number $[MQ]$ and composition $\dfrac{[MQP]}{[MQ]}$, we can not only infer inductively that the population probably has approximately the composition $\dfrac{[MQP]}{[MQ]}$ but can state the degree of probability and approximation. With it on hand, conjoined with the more pedestrian articles of the probability calculus, we can hope to justify all the so-called 'methods of science' as applications of a logic no less abstract, formal, and necessary, although much more intricate, than the procedures of the mathematician. Since the principle is purely logical, presupposing nothing about its data or its objects except that they be members of classes — a status which no conceivable entities could avoid — it makes induction quite independent of any supposed maxims of uniformity, causation, or sufficient reason, and valid alike for a world of metaphysical atoms, or of organic interfusions, or of necessary connections. It hence proves the jurisdiction of inductive procedure over all the branches of philosophy as well as over the natural sciences, the professions, and common sense, and it guarantees the relevance of the content of any one of these fields to all the rest.

These are large claims, but they are the least claims which a solution of the problem of induction can make without confessing its entire incompetence. An inductive principle not adequate to metaphysics must have material presuppositions, but a principle which has material presuppositions must itself depend upon induction for its substantiation.

Our theory has, I have argued, the massiveness, simplicity, and primitiveness, and even the margin of indefiniteness, which the philosopher would expect for such a fundamental problem. The probabilities which in fact it imputes to specific inductions are closely in accord with both psychological habit and careful scientific usage, far surpassing the much too little which the skeptics allow, but reassuringly inferior to the much too much which dogmatic rationalists and traditionalists have asked or offered. Its method is purely extensional, counting actual individuals and requiring no weighing of analogies, no intuition of organic fitness, and no canvassing of bodiless or transcendent possibilities. Most of the objections which it provokes prove on examination to be dissatisfactions with the bare notion of logical connection or of probability, and can be dispersed by a reminder of what logic and probability are. Misgivings, for example, concerning the possibility of unfair selection and demonic interference must be quieted by an understanding that this is but a corollary, discounted in advance by the sampling law, of the truism that highly probable propositions may nevertheless be false.

Though in principle assured of our analysis of induction, by a rich convergence of evidence as well as by the abstract and original force of arithmetic, we shall still do well to claim no finality for this edition of it. The main thesis and my defense are at best in need of amendment and supplement, both in mathematical and logical detail and in philosophic context, and they invite correction, I have no doubt, with respect to downright errors of expression and idea. Some few of the gaps or apparent gaps in the epistemological theory of the matter we have already acknowledged. The necessary revisions, and the development of a complete and systematic logic of induction, are duties which I confidently recommend to philosophers of seriousness and good will.

INDEX

Additive law, 49, 60, 79, 81, 82, 93
Adjunction, 34 and n., 49
Affirming the consequent, 3, 112, 114
Alexander, 170
Alternation, 35
Ampliative inference, 11–12, 80, 125, 133, 136, 137, 200 n.
Analogy, 53, 113, 117–118, 162, 193, 203
Analysis, logical, 9–10, 51, 91, 131, 138, 171, 178, 181–182, 186; as aid to generalization, 120–121
Analytic propositions, 9–10, 25, 26, 46, 78, 102, 130, 138, 139, 161, 181, 188, 202
Animal faith, 16, 17, 54, 133, 185, 200
Animal induction, 3, 165, 183
Antecedent probability, 113
Anticipations of this theory, 195 ff., esp. 197, 201
Approximation, inductive: absolute vs. relative, 85, 87 n., 96; and degree of probability, 85–87, 91–92, 100, 106, 143, 160, 197–198, 202
A priori, 25, 93, 94, 98, 102, 124, 129–130, 132, 138, 143, 154, 172 n., 180–182
A priori probabilities, 160, 192
Aristotle, 5, 6, 7, 39 n., 53, 121, 155, 170, 187
Artificial illustrations of inductive principles, value of, 80, 95–96, 121, 148, 188
Association, psychological, 164, 168, 170; statistical, 7, 68, 70, 118, 120, 141, 146, 147, 187, 192–193
Assumption that induction is valid, 14, 187
Atomism and induction, 170, 172–173, 202
Averages, induction of, 109; 'law' of, 63
Ayer, 185 n.

Bacon, 16 n., 122, 123 and n., 189
Bad luck, 62, 170
Barbara, 7, 24, 27, 28, 30, 32, 36, 37, 38, 80, 102, 106
Bayes, 55
Bayes' theorem, 113–116, 130, 171; in induction, 191
Belief, 5, 18, 30, 31, 39, 41, 55, 58, 134–135, 145, 152, 164, 170, 185
Bergmann, 55 n.
Bergson, 173
Bernoulli's principle, 63, 85, 190; inversion of, 87, 190–191, 196, 200
Bertrand's paradox, 73
Bias, 66–67; in induction, 140
Binomial theorem, 181
Bosanquet, 51, 122 n., 193 and n.
Bridgman, 55
Broad, 110, 153, 155, 166 n., 189 n., 192 n., 193 and n.
Butler, 53 and n., 133

Campbell, 17 and n., 182 n.
Carnap, 55 n., 110, 192 n., 193
'Cases', favorable and possible, 8, 36, 49, 50–51, 71, 73, 147
Causal laws, induction of, 108, 118, 171; conditioned, 108
Causation and confirmation of inductive conclusion, 121, 164–165
Causation, law of, 153, 187, 202
Cause and effect, 108, 136, 153, 174–175, 187, 188
Celarent, 36, 80, 106
Certainty, 9, 14, 33, 36, 44, 59, 69, 91, 106, 142, 154; not obtainable by compounding probabilities, 61, 63, 69; not obtainable in induction, 14, 31, 54, 79, 91, 106–107, 123 n., 134, 136 n., 137, 140, 149, 186, 188, 189, 191, 195, 201
Changing populations, 155
Changing probabilities, 45, 67, 73, 115, 126 n., 141–144
Chaos, induction in, 161, 195

Posit, 62
Positivism, 128–129, 130, 133, 134, 158 n., 175, 185
Possibilities, pure, not required to ground induction, 40, 203; improbable, no bar to inductive validity, 63, 66, 143, 145–146, 149–152, 203
Possible compositions of population, range of, 88, 94; hypostatization of, 160, 190, 200 n.; prior probabilities of, 99, 160, 192 and n., 200 n.
Possible experience, 158 n., 177, 200
'Possible inferences', 38–40, 60–61, 197; two senses of, 39, 199; inductive, 104, 138, 199 and n.
Possible universes, 200 n.
Pragmatism, 16, 124, 127, 130, 155, 156 n., 158 n., 173, 175, 185, 186
Predesignation, 116, 162
Prediction, 6–7, 12, 108, 110, 111, 121, 155–156 and n., 161, 171, 175, 185; as test, 113–114, 127
Premise and conclusion, 5, 28–29, 102, 126, 197; inductive, 11, 31, 137–138, 178–179, 193, 197
Presuppositions of induction, alleged, 139–162, 169, 172, 176, 181, 197–198, 199–200 and n., 201, 202
Previous knowledge, the rôle of, in hypothesis, 113–114; — in induction, 117–119, 146
Primitive propositions and terms, 25, 58, 122, 181–182
Principium individuationis, 74
Probability, 8, 12, 14, 20, 32–76, 137, 141, 152, 201; logic, mathematics, and calculus of, 8, 14, 32–33, 48, 51, 56, 67, 107, 114–116, 133–134, 197, 202; its analogies with entailment and inconsistency, 36, 40, 46, 50, 58, 63, 74–75, 137, 152, 187, 195, 197, 201; its contrasts with entailment and inconsistency, 45–47, 58–59, 62, 76, 126 n., 137, 152 n., 197, 201, 203; relativity of, 44–47, 67, 71–73, 115, 126 n., 141–143; 'the', 44–45, 60, 68, 71–72, 162; objectivity of, — *see* Objectivity; theories of, 50–56, 64–65, 134, 193, 196
Probability: of frequencies; of matching samples; of maturity. *See*

Frequencies, Matching, Maturity, *respectively*
Probability connection: between subject and predicate, 188, 193; between sample and population, 189, 193
'Probability laws', 63, 107
Probable error, 87, 197
Process and induction, 155–156, 173–174, 194
Product, logical, 12 n., 78
Profit: of rationality, 30, 59, 62, 127, 134–135, 162; of probability, 59, 62, 162; of truth, 5, 30, 59
Proof, 125–126, 131; and discovery, 126; and persuasion, 131
Properties, 6 and n., 12 and n., 73, 113, 138–139, 160, 175, 177–178, 181, 192; determinate and indeterminate, 160–161; relational, 108, 111; spectrum of, 73
Proportional laws, 7, 9, 106–107; predominance of, 41, 188
Proportional syllogism, 8, 11–13, 21, 35, 37–41, 47, 51, 54, 56, 76, 79, 81, 93, 106, 137, 162, 198, 201; of second level, in induction, 21, 93, 98–100, 102, 132, 201–202
Propositional functions, 28
Propositions, 24 and n., 39–41, 47, 73, 136 n., 175
Protosamples, 21, 93, 97, 98, 101, 104, 142–143, 196, 201
Pseudoproblems, supposed, 16, 133, 185
Psychology of inference, 3, 5, 30–31, 55–56, 58, 126, 145; inductive, 15, 121, 134, 163–165, 183, 185, 203
Pythagoras, 14

Quantum, 119, 120, 158
Quine, 7
Quotation marks, vi–vii, 136 n.

Ramsey, 55
Randomness, vi, 54–55, 66–67, 69–70; in induction, 140, 144–145, 150, 167, 198
Random sampling, 119, 144, 146, 147
Rationalists, 182, 187–188, 203
Raw feels, 180
'Real causation', 153, 187, 200
Realism, 128, 169–170